Welcome, husband in pursuit.

Today marks the first day of the rest of your life
pursuing your wife.

It won't always be easy, but she is well worth the fight.

The 31 Day Pursuit
CHALLENGE

HUSBAND
IN PURSUIT

31 DAILY CHALLENGES

FOR LOVING YOUR WIFE WELL

By Ryan Frederick

LION PRESS
TACOMA, WASHINGTON

HUSBAND IN PURSUIT

31 Daily Challenges for Loving Your Wife Well

Copyright © 2017 by Ryan and Selena Frederick

Published by Lion Press
a division of Vilicus LLC

Second Edition

Author portrait by Julie Cannon. Used with permission.

ISBN-10: 0-9974713-2-8

ISBN-13: 978-0-9974713-2-8

(pbk. bw.)

2 3 4 5 6 7 8 9   APB   28 27 26 25 24 23 22

Printed in the United States of America

This book is dedicated to my dad,
an avid husband in pursuit.

Thank you for loving mom so well.

Contents

A Letter from the Author

A perfect man would never act from a sense of duty; he'd always want the right thing more than the wrong one. Duty is only a substitute for love (of God and of other people) like a crutch which is a substitute for a leg. Most of us need the crutch at times; but of course it is idiotic to use the crutch when our own legs (our own loves, tastes, habits etc.) can do the journey on their own.

C. S. Lewis

This book is a crutch by design. And as C. S. Lewis pointed out, a crutch is a tool, not a substitute for what it supports. A tool like this can never replace your love for your wife, but it can help strengthen it and give you time to grow. In a perfect world—and if we were perfect men—we would never need a book like this to spur us along in pursuit of our wives. We'd readily love and pursue our brides as we should and as they deserve: selflessly, consistently, and in ways that connect most with their hearts. I'm still waiting for that perfect world to materialize. Until then, give me more Jesus, more help, and all the wisdom you can spare.

Part of getting off crutches is developing the strength necessary to stand on your own. Recently I've picked up the hobby of lifting weights in the morning with a few good friends. It's mostly an excuse to get out of the house, hang out with guys I care about, and stay somewhat fit in the process. Just about every weekday, we meet at 6:00 a.m. and lift for about ninety minutes. The timeframe stays the same, but results vary. When I push hard, I get sore and my muscles get stronger. When I slack off and socialize too much, I don't get as good of a workout and my time isn't as effective. Socializing isn't bad, but if I want to get the most out of the time spent in the gym, I must apply myself. The time will pass either way, the only difference is the end result. This is why we follow workout plans to keep things on track.

The same is true for this 31-Day Pursuit Challenge. Thirty-one days will pass whether you read this book or not, and whether you apply its principles or not. The question is, how different will you be after that time? How different will your relationship with your wife be? How much deeper will your understanding of the gospel be?

ARE YOU UP FOR THE CHALLENGE?

Consider yourself warned. The next thirty-one days won't be easy. That's why it's called a challenge! It's meant to be difficult. It will require new honesty with yourself and your wife. It will require work—real work—some that you won't want to do. You'll be asked to act selflessly, plan dates, take the time to express what's in your heart and mind, ask yourself hard questions, and go out of your way to show your wife you love her. Real change is never cheap. The cheapest aspect of this book is the price tag! The cost goes up from here. In short, this challenge will cost you time, energy, thought, and cash (though how much cash largely depends on you). You will need fortitude and determination if you're to finish this journey well.

If you accept this challenge, it won't be cheap but it *will* be worth it! I can assure you that your effort won't be in vain. If you apply yourself—if you lift the weight—you will grow, your marriage will grow, and your wife will experience your love in new ways.

WHAT SHOULD YOU EXPECT?

Now is a good time to calibrate your expectations. I encourage you to approach this book with one agenda: to extravagantly express your love to your wife, regardless of how she responds. I don't recommend you read it with the intent of getting your wife to do something you want her to do or become someone you want her to be. Chances are good that she will respond positively—love often has that effect. But depending on your exact circumstances, she may respond slowly or not at all. Pursue her anyway—it's how Christ pursues us every day. Rest in that truth.

There's no way I can predict or guarantee how this book or the 31-Day Pursuit Challenge will affect your marriage. I wish I could! However, I can give you three promises:

1. It won't be easy, but it will be worth it.
2. It won't fix your marriage, but Jesus can.
3. If you complete every day, you *will* grow.

WHAT DO I EXPECT FROM YOU?

If you've read this introduction and you still choose to proceed, I'll assume you've totally bought in. From here on out, you and I are in this together. Every devotional was written and each pursuit challenge was created with *you* and your bride in mind—along with a few assumptions about what you will bring to the table.

I expect effort. I'm happy to put in the time to create this book. All I ask for in return is that you start strong, finish well, and don't cut corners. I'd ask the same if we were in the gym together—if we're going to do this thing, let's do it well. Let's not waste each other's time.

I expect consistency. Now is the time to mentally set aside intentional and undistracted moments each day to study and reflect. Do the good work of pursuit—of God and your wife. Pray, read, absorb, write, think, and act without reservation.

I expect honesty. Along the way, be honest with yourself, with God, and with your wife.

Enough preamble, let's get started. I can't wait to see how God acts in your life and in your marriage. To him be all the glory!

Onward,

P. S. I'm praying for you and your marriage—that you will flourish in the hope and joy only available in Christ. Rest in him throughout this journey. He is enough! (2 Peter 1:3)

Challenge Accepted

I, _____ , *accept this challenge.*
YOUR NAME

I understand that pursuing my wife won't always be easy, but she is always worth the fight.

I realize that it is only by God's grace that I am loved in Christ, and it will only be through God's grace that I grow and learn to love my wife as he intends.

Finally, I understand that my wife is a gift from God and it is my duty, honor, and privilege to love her as Christ loves the church.

_____
SIGNATURE

_____
DATE

The 31 Day Pursuit
CHALLENGE

We love because
he first loved us.

1 JOHN 4:19

Before You Start

You might find it helpful to know how each day is structured:

SCRIPTURE

Each day starts with a passage from the Bible. Read it well. Nothing will transform your heart more than carefully reading God's Word and letting it read you.

DEVOTIONAL CONTENT

The devotionals draw connecting lines between the gospel and married life—to help you discern the character and will of God, experience his love, and apply it to how you pursue your wife.

REFLECTION QUESTIONS

Each day includes a few questions to help you process the day's content and apply it to the pursuit challenge. The quality of your experience depends on how much effort you put in. Take time to answer honestly and thoroughly—it could pay off for years.

PRAYER

There are short prayer prompts to help get you started with

prayers of your own. I recommend writing a few sentences of prayer each day in the space provided as a way of journaling your ongoing dialogue with God.

DAILY PURSUITS

The pursuit challenges are what make this experience unique. Each one is meant to help you pursue your wife in new ways. Some challenges are hard and involved, others are fast and fun. Resolve now to complete each one to the best of your ability.

ICONS

Each pursuit has clock and dollar icons to give you a rough idea of how much time and money you can expect to spend *relative to the other daily pursuits*. Exactly how much time and money you spend will always depend on you.

FIELD NOTES

Jot down any revelations, thoughts, or observations about how the pursuit went or how your wife responded. This will help you learn from your experience and improve in the future.

HEADS-UP!

You'll see *heads-up* prompts on some of the days. They allow you to plan for pursuits that are more involved. Heed them and it will go well with you. Remember: planning is part of the pursuit.

A man doesn't own his marriage; he is only the steward of his wife's love.

ED COLE

1

Pursuing Her as You Are Pursued

Husbands, love your wives, as Christ loved the church and gave himself up for her . . . In the same way husbands should love their wives as their own bodies. He who loves his wife loves himself. For no one ever hated his own flesh, but nourishes and cherishes it, just as Christ does the church, because we are members of his body.

Ephesians 5:25, 28–30

I love fixing things. We have a glass sliding door that goes out to our back deck, and for the longest time it was obnoxiously noisy and difficult to open. One Saturday morning I finally got fed up with how dysfunctional it was, so I resolved to find the problem and fix it once and for all. I pulled the door off its track and looked underneath to see what the issue was. Sure enough, the wheel bearings were completely shot. So I packed our oldest daughter into the car and headed to the hardware store. After some searching we finally found what we needed. We bought the parts, headed home, and fixed the door. Done. It was a simple, tangible, rewarding job! I must have slid the door open and closed twenty times that day just to feel it glide smoothly and quietly along the track.

As men, it's generally true that we like to fix things; and we're pretty good at it! Just find the problem, figure out a solution, and take action. Done and done. Unfortunately, marriage isn't quite that simple. Problems in marriage often present themselves as superficial, but their roots actually go much deeper. If we're not careful, we apply the same fix-it logic we use to repair household problems and expect everything to be resolved. Then, if and when problems persist, we're confused. *I did what she wanted, so why is she still upset?* Often the thing we're focused on fixing isn't the primary issue; it's just a symptom.

It's tempting in a book like this one to prescribe things for you to do, all with a fix-it mindset: *Do more of this and that so your marriage looks and functions how it should.* It is true that you are called to love your wife in tangible, visible ways. You are undoubtedly called to love your bride as Christ loved the church and that sort of love has real actions associated with it. But loving and pursuing your wife well starts with knowing how you're loved and pursued by Christ. The better you understand how you're loved by Christ, the better you'll love your wife. Christ's love always starts in you and flows outward through you.

Today marks the start of your journey of learning how to pursue your bride more intentionally. But first, I need to level with you: I want this book to be more than a collection of ideas and to-dos. If you finish the next thirty-one days without a deeper understanding of who Christ is, I will have missed the mark.

My prayer is that we can journey together and explore how profoundly and recklessly we're loved by Jesus, and from there, be transformed from the inside out in how we love our wives. I use the phrase "journey together" intentionally. I may be writing this book, but I assure you I'm also learning as I go. Most of all, I need daily reminders of the gospel—the profound assurance that I am loved by God through Christ. From there, I simply need tools to help me be more intentional as a husband.

As you and I journey together, let us not forget that the key to loving our wives "as Christ loved the church" starts with understanding exactly how Christ actively loves us. From that understanding the actions of love—*the pursuit*—will naturally follow.

REFLECT

How has Christ loved the church? How has he pursued you?

PRAY

Pray for soft hearts for you and your wife throughout this journey.

Pursuit 1

ACT

⊙⊙⊙ | $$$

Find and write down at least three verses that illustrate how you are loved and pursued by Christ. Then explain in your own words how being pursued by Christ influences how you can pursue your wife. It may take some research to find specific verses but that's a good thing. Embrace the challenge. Decide today to pursue your wife with everything you've got.

___ *Check here when you've completed this pursuit.*

FIELD NOTES

Thoughts, feelings, or observations about today's pursuit?

Ephesians 5:25 - Husbands Love your wives as
Christ loved the church + gave himself up for her

Eph 5:33 However, let each of you love his wife as
himself, + let the wife see that she a respects her
husband

1 Peter - husbands Live w/your wives in an understanding way
Showing honor To the woman as the weaker vessel Since

HEADS-UP! they are heirs with you of the grace
of life, So that your prayers may not be hindered

This may seem early, but you might want to start planning for Day 31 (it's a big one). Feel free to take a look ahead.

DAY

2

Seeing Her as Christ Sees Her

While we were still weak, at the right time Christ died for the
ungodly. For one will scarcely die for a righteous person—though
perhaps for a good person one would dare even to die—but God
shows His love for us in that while we were still sinners,
Christ died for us.

ROMANS 5:6–8

Our church recently held baptisms during a Sunday gathering. Two eight-year-old kids had decided to publicly declare their faith in Christ. As our pastor introduced each one, he gave them a chance to read a verse that had influenced their lives. As the children read their verses, my mind wandered. I longed for and dreamed of the day I'd get to see my two daughters publicly share their decisions to follow Jesus. Tears filled my eyes and a knot formed in the back of my throat.

My daydream continued. I began to envision them as teenagers, then as young women. I imagined them introducing me to boys they liked—as it stands, I doubt if any will be good enough for either of them. Eventually I began wondering what kind of men each of my daughters would marry. Would their future husbands treat them well? Would they speak to them kindly, gently, and lovingly? Would they respect my daughters and treasure them as I do? Would they lead and love them sacrificially as Christ loved his bride, the church?

Then I felt convicted as my questioning turned inward.

Do I respect and treasure my wife as God does? Do I speak to her kindly, gently, and lovingly? Do I pursue her as he does? The conviction was deep, and it still feels fresh as I write this.

It's sobering to think of your bride as a daughter of God. Yes, in Christ, you are also adopted into God's family and called a son, but have you ever thought of yourself as God's son-in-law? I can't help but picture him standing at the front door, shotgun in hand, warning me to have his baby girl home before 10:00 p.m. Sounds ridiculous, but perhaps it's a useful image to remind you that your wife is God's precious daughter.

One of the mixed blessings of marriage is familiarity. I say *mixed* because there are two very different sides to the same coin. On one side, you can be closer and more vulnerable with your wife than with any other person. On the other side, you can grow too familiar and get lazy with each other. I'm not just talking about using the bathroom with the door open or forgetting common courtesies once practiced while dating. (Side note: It's a good idea to maintain a healthy amount of decorum in your marriage out of mutual respect). The biggest downside to familiarity is forgetfulness: forgetting what makes your wife remarkable, forgetting why you were drawn to her in the first place, and forgetting just how special she is in God's eyes.

We can learn the most about familiarity from looking at the way God treats it. No one is more familiar with you than God. He knitted you together in your mother's womb (Psalm 139:13), he knows the number of hairs on your head (even if it decreases daily) (Luke 12:7), and he knows exactly what you do, think, say, and intend, every moment of every day (Psalm 139:2). Nothing about you is a mystery or a surprise to God. Yet he loves. He forgives. And despite how much you neglect him, he is ready to meet you wherever you are and pour out everything he promises without delay. In Christ, you have all the benefits of familiarity and none of the drawbacks. That's what it means to be called son. That's the good news of the gospel!

Experiencing the truth of the gospel will forever change how you view your wife. Christ views her with the same loving, long-suffering, patient, and kind eyes with which he views you. He adores her! She is his little girl, all grown up. He knew her in the womb, designed her in his image, and entrusted her into your care. Your bride is God's daughter first and your wife second. Remember to treasure her as God does, and love her as Christ has loved the church.

REFLECT

Take a step back and think about what makes your wife remarkable as a daughter of God. Why did you pursue her in the first place?

Ambition
Work Ethic

PRAY

Ask the Holy Spirit to reveal areas where you've grown too familiar with your bride. Ask for wisdom in how to love her well as a daughter of the King.

Pursuit 2

ACT

◑◑◑ | $ $ $

Grab a pen and paper. Handwrite a letter to your wife and list at least ten things you love about her. Leave it somewhere she'll find it, or read it to her out loud over dinner.

✓
___ *Check here when you've completed this pursuit.*

FIELD NOTES

Thoughts, feelings, or observations about today's pursuit?

How grateful I am our have Spent 20 yrs Together. Really That she has put up with me for 20 years.

HEADS-UP!

You may want to let your wife know that tomorrow will be "an experiment in antiquity." Take a look ahead; warn her if needed.

DAY

3

An Experiment
in Antiquity

Look carefully then how you walk, not as unwise but as wise,
making the best use of the time, because the days are evil.
Therefore do not be foolish, but understand what the
will of the Lord is.

Ephesians 5:15–17

One of the biggest tension points in our household is our phones. If I'm not careful with my usage, Selena feels like she's constantly fighting for my attention. Even if I've turned off all notifications to alleviate the problem, I still find myself checking e-mail and texts incessantly. In many ways my phone a lifeline because it allows me to monitor and respond to work-related tasks and ultimately earn an income, but that's no excuse. She usually vocalizes her frustration if I'm distracted when she's trying to talk to me. Depending on the timing and my blood-sugar level, I can get defensive, and suddenly we're arguing. In my defense, I'm not the sole offender; our roles are often reversed.

You know how it is, and you can probably empathize.

So much of our lives revolve around the Internet. It's a useful tool, but like any tool it can be misused. When it is, it invades our most precious moments and contaminates sacred time together as a family. Because of our propensity to be drawn to our devices, we've had to create clear, immovable boundaries. Whenever we're on a date, we leave all technology in the car (except, now that we have kids, Selena will keep her phone nearby and on silent in case our baby-sitter calls). Dinner time is totally unplugged so we can engage in meaningful conversation with each other and our kids. Mornings are reserved for time with God and breakfast with each other. Only after we've all connected can I grab my phone and dive into work.

There's a reason Paul instructed the Ephesian church in today's verse to "make the best use of the time" by reminding them to "not be foolish" and to understand the will of God. They experienced the same propensity for distraction that we feel today. Distraction is a human problem, not a technology problem. For the Ephesians, we can see what was going on by reading the surrounding context in the first half of chapter five. Paul warned them against sexual immorality, covetousness, foolish talk, and crude joking. But Paul's instruction wasn't just about telling them what not to do; it was about urging them toward the right pursuit.

Other translations, like the King James Version, use the phrase, "redeeming the time" instead of "making the best use of the time." The Greek words behind that phrase can be literally translated as "buying up for yourselves the opportunity."[1] The opportunity for what, exactly? To be wise. To learn the will of God and pursue it, and as it says a few verses later, to build each other up with "psalms, hymns, and spiritual songs" and sing "to the Lord with your heart" (Ephesians 5:19).

Paul had a rightful a sense of urgency. Life is short and the gospel is huge. There is much work to be done for the glory of God! But as humans we tend to drift toward foolish, idle talk—toward distraction—when so much is at stake. Paul's words weren't instructions to work for salvation, but rather an encouragement to live in full light of the gospel they had received!

Paul's instructions have direct implications for our marriages. We are called to steward our moments wisely and caution our hearts against meaningless, fruitless distractions. We're called to speak intentionally, not foolishly or with crude talk. Finally, we're called to lead our families to do the same.

Imagine yourself twenty years from now. What will you celebrate more: checking your phone as much as you do, or spending quality moments with your bride? Heed Paul's wisdom: "Look carefully then how you walk, not as unwise but as wise, making the best use of the time."

REFLECT

Do technology and other distractions steal from your quality time as a couple? What's one recent example when this happened?

What aspects of technology consume the largest portion of your time (apps, TV, websites, devices, other)? How can you use them more wisely?

PRAY

Ask God for an eternal perspective of technology and for help to make the best use of your time. Pray for the Holy Spirit to reveal areas where you can improve.

ACT

☺☺☺ | $ $ $

Today's challenge is an experiment in antiquity. Imagine civilization before electricity was invented. People sat, talked, read, and experienced life so vividly—*so presently*—without distraction.

Remove all distractions for a day or an evening. Turn off screens, cancel activities, and if you're feeling radical, switch off the breakers. Then spend time together. Play a game, sit and talk, and just be present. Explain what you're doing and let her know it's your time to connect on new levels.

(If your wife is doing her own version of the 31-Day Pursuit Challenge, she'll be doing a similar pursuit today.)

___ *Check here when you've completed this pursuit.*

FIELD NOTES

Thoughts, feelings, or observations about today's pursuit?

DAY

4

A Prayerful Pursuit

*Thus says the LORD who made the earth, the LORD who formed
it to establish it—the LORD is his name: Call to me and I will
answer you, and will tell you great and hidden things
that you have not known.*

JEREMIAH 33:2–3

Praying has always been a challenge for me. It may be because
I'm not a natural communicator; I tend to think about and
internalize things much more quickly than I talk about them—if
I ever do. There have been countless times when Selena and I are
talking and she explains a situation to me and asks me for input.
She'll ask questions almost rhetorically and continue processing
vocally until another question arises. After a while, she'll stop
and ask abruptly, "Are you even listening?" I almost always am,
but I catch myself answering her questions in my head. She often
sees my mind working and lovingly reminds me, "I can't hear

what you're thinking!"

Praying is a discipline I constantly have to work on. But I don't think my personality is the issue; it's my pride. Praying is only necessary when one actually worships and relies on God. Why go to God if you don't worship him or need his help?

For a long time, I excused my lack of a prayer life because I thought, *God and I have an understanding.* I figured that if he promised or said something, that was that. Why go back to him and ask him to rehash what he already said? I was arrogant and foolish. It's like the wife who complained to her husband for not telling her he loved her enough, to which he replied, "I told you I loved you the day we got married, and if something changes I'll let you know!" What kind of relationship is that?

I wrongly believed prayer to be superfluous to a trusting relationship with God. I assumed that his promises, though unchanging, didn't require a response from me. Perhaps I didn't want to bother God; but more tragically, maybe I didn't see the value in conversing with him.

Of all the verses in the Bible about prayer, why refer to Jeremiah 33:3 in today's Scripture? I believe it's jarring and thrilling in a unique way. Jeremiah is called the "weeping prophet" because all his prophetic writings tell of God's impending judgment on Judah. Being God's mouthpiece didn't exonerate him from feeling sorrow for the nation he loved. Knowing that is part of what makes this verse so exciting! As a man reading this, I hope you feel the same way.

This particular verse begins a chapter in which God reiterated his promises to his people. He reminded them that he would fulfill his covenant with David. He reminded them that he would cleanse and forgive them, restore their fortunes and abundance. And he reminds them that Jesus—their Savior—was still to come. When God said he would tell them of "great and hidden things" that they had not known when they called on him, he was reminding them to rest in his promises and his character. He was calling them to remember that he was God—ruler over all, King over every great and hidden mystery.

God calls us in the same way today. He wants us to call on his name and watch in wonder as he plays his role . . . *as God*. This is why we pray: to commune with God, remind ourselves of his promises, and worship him as the one true God of everything.

Prayer is essential to a vibrant relationship with God, and it's just as vital to healthy marriage. Praying for and with your bride will unify and strengthen you in your reliance on God. Prayer brings you closer to God and deepens your understanding of who God is, who your wife is, and who you are. Conversing with the Creator of the universe is a powerful privilege that Jesus' death provided for us. As a husband, you have a unique responsibility and role in leading your family to the feet of God in prayer. Make prayer a priority—both personally and as a family—and watch in wonder as God moves in your lives in great and unknown ways.

REFLECT

Recall one time when prayer has strengthened you as an individual and together as a couple. Why do you think praying to God strengthened you in that situation?

How can you intentionally pray *for* and *with* your wife?

PRAY

Pray for wisdom and ways to make prayer more a part of your lives. Ask God for help to lead well in this area.

ACT   ☻☻☻ | $ $ $

Pray together tonight before going to bed. Ask your wife what's on her heart, and discuss God's promises together. Then, agree with her as you pray together.

Take the lead and thank God for everything he is doing in your wife, your lives, and your marriage. Make sure to hold hands as a symbol of unity and agreement.

___ *Check here when you've completed this pursuit.*

FIELD NOTES

Thoughts, feelings, or observations about today's pursuit?

5

The Original Reckless Pursuit

The kingdom of heaven is like treasure hidden in a field, which
a man found and covered up. Then in his joy he goes and sells
all that he has and buys that field.
Again, the kingdom of heaven is like a merchant in search of
fine pearls, who, on finding one pearl of great value, went and
sold all that he had and bought it.

MATTHEW 13:44–46

I always knew I wanted to marry Selena—I was just unsure of the details. When I asked her to be my wife I had very little else in mind. Details . . . Where would we live and how would we pay rent? Would we finish school? If so, how? None of that mattered when I decided to propose. Nothing mattered more to me than she did.

So I sold my car and bought a ring (it wasn't a very expensive car). By God's grace she agreed to marry me! I wasn't completely unprepared—at least not mentally. I knew we'd figure things out and that it would be challenging at first. I just had nothing physical to show for my mental preparedness. No money, no job, nothing.

Looking back, I now realize what was happening. Selena was (and still is) my ultimate treasure aside from Jesus. I was like the men Jesus described who found hidden treasure and a fine pearl, then sold everything they had to get them. Selena is my treasure. I wanted to spend my life with this girl; I wanted to show her how much I loved her. Marriage was the only way to do that.

I realize that Jesus wasn't referring to marriage in Matthew 13, but the underlying principle is profound and applicable. He was illustrating the idea of value, the concept of perceived worth, and the remote chance of finding such a rare and coveted discovery. Namely, he was talking about the cost, value, and opportunity of salvation.

The transactions Jesus described sound radical to you and me today—*How can I possibly give up everything?*—but I assure you, they're completely rational. Jesus' message would have resonated with the disciples in ways we don't readily understand today. In Jesus' time, acquiring and storing wealth was complicated. There were no banks, and one faced a constant risk of losing everything one owned to war, theft, or the government. As a result, property owners consolidated their wealth by purchasing small, valuable items—like jewels and pearls—that could be easily concealed. They would then hide these items by burying them in the ground or placing them in notches of trees or other hiding places.

It wasn't unusual for a wealthy person to die abruptly only to leave undiscovered, undisclosed, and unclaimed riches behind. Men would search for lost and hidden treasures in hopes of striking it rich, much like we see today with the lottery, the Texas oil boom, the California gold rush, and every reality TV show you've ever seen. When he spoke of the treasure and the fine pearls, Jesus was referring to a cultural norm to communicate truth about God's kingdom: hearing the gospel is like discovering the most valuable treasure possible! It's ours to have, but we must trust Jesus entirely—we must trust that God's kingdom is worth it. As followers of Christ, that means we die to ourselves and live unto him. We're called to be living sacrifices (Romans 12:1) who die daily to flesh and live new life in him (Galatians 5:24).

Following Jesus—truly trusting him—only makes sense once we understand the limitless worth of what he offers and the miracle of him making it available. To hear the gospel and not turn to Christ is akin to finding a hidden treasure in a field, covering it up with dirt, and going about life as if nothing happened. There is no greater treasure in this life or eternity than God's kingdom, and Jesus paid its cost. He bought it by his blood on the cross. Not only that, but God also revealed to us where to find his kingdom: by grace alone through faith alone in Christ alone. It's a miracle that you've even *heard* the gospel—it's like you've been given precise GPS coordinates to the most valuable treasure on earth.

Christ recklessly pursued you through the cross because of his great love and desire for unhindered relationship with you. It is your divine adoption—your identity as a rescued and redeemed son of God—that empowers you to love your wife "as Christ loved the church" (Ephesians 5:25).

God loves you and wants a relationship with you just as he wants you to love your bride and pursue a relationship with her. In your role as a husband, building your relationship with your bride is your singular calling. As you pursue your wife, consider the men who sold everything they had and sought treasure. How do you do that in your relationship with your wife? You put everything on the line—your time, your attention, your intentional actions. You seek her by actively building your relationship, or digging in the field to find the treasure that is your growth together. Today's pursuit is part of turning over new ground by having new experiences together.

REFLECT

What experiences with your wife have built your relationship the most? Think of two or three and list them below.

working through challenges as a team

Doing Life Together

Why do you think those experiences stand out?

Teamwork

PRAY

Ask God for openness in conversation, for reminders of Christ's pursuit, and for help in seeking new experiences that will deepen your appreciation of each other.

ACT

⏱⏱⏱ | $ $ $

Plan a new experience with your wife and surprise her with it. Be creative! It need not be expensive (though it's fine if it is), but it must be something new that neither of you have ever done. Either set a date on the calendar, plan it for today, or create a coupon for one new experience (redeemable in the next few weeks).

Whatever you choose to do, don't delay! Plan something, do it, and make a new memory together.

____ *Check here when you've completed this pursuit.*

FIELD NOTES

Thoughts, feelings, or observations about today's pursuit?

HEADS-UP!

Ask your bride to set aside two hours tomorrow. You can look ahead to learn why, but don't tell her what it's for.

DAY

6

Into the Wild

*When Jesus heard this, he withdrew from there in a boat to a
desolate place by himself . . . and after he had dismissed the
crowds, he went up on the mountain by himself to pray. When
evening came, he was there alone.*

MATTHEW 14:13, 23

Having a morning routine is like an anchor for my day. But
all too often I'm content skipping what matters most: time
with God. If I oversleep or grab my phone too quickly, I'll lose
track of time and get caught up with whatever tasks are on my
plate for the day. I may read a verse somewhere online or say
a half-hearted prayer, but it's never as focused or in-depth as a
morning quiet time—it never fills me up. So I begin to coast
down the road of life; I shift out of gear, drop it into neutral,
and let my momentum carry me forward. All seems fine as I
reminisce about memories of intimacy with God, all the while
sliding steadily into self-reliance. If enough time passes, I'll settle

into a new morning routine that excludes dedicated time with God entirely. Eventually I crash and burn. Life gets hilly, my momentum slows, and soon I roll backward or career off the road entirely. It's not a cycle I'm proud of, but it's the truth.

Today's passages are bookends around Jesus miraculously feeding five thousand people (probably more) with only five loaves of bread and two fish. As we read, we get a strong sense of Jesus' reliance on the Father. He was depleted and in need of restoration. If Jesus, who was fully God and fully man, needed exclusive time with God, how much more do we? How much more does your wife?

The people of God need to hear his voice. A day without Scripture and prayer does to your soul what a day without water does to your physical body. Yesterday's portion may sustain you for a little while, but you will inevitably grow thirsty and dry—you will die. God graciously built rhythms and cycles into life: sleep to refresh the body and seasons to reset the earth.

When the Israelites traversed the desert, God provided daily bread—manna from heaven—for their sustenance (Psalm 78:24). Every morning they were tasked with gathering only enough for that day; any extra would rot. God could have easily provided a less perishable food source, so why didn't he? He understood their need for daily dependence on him. Just as I do, they constantly battled self-reliance. The perishable manna was another one of God's sovereign acts of love and pursuit designed to keep God's people close—to hold their hands through the desert, despite their childish protests and insistence on independence. Our God knows we need him daily.

God is pursuing your heart, as a man and as a husband, every time he lets you reach the end of yourself. Your limits are God-designed! They're a call to the wilderness—to stop, pray, read God's Word, and commune with him. Your spiritual hunger, tiredness, and thirst are all constant reminders of your desperate need for Jesus. When you're tired, rest in God's sovereignty. When you're worried, trust in God's peace. When you're losing patience, remember God's patient and active love in Christ. And when you're thirsty and dry, run to the well of God's Word and find refreshment in Christ's living water. It's one of God's greatest graces to allow us to grow tired and hungry daily! We need constant reminding of our limitations so we learn to trust in our limitless God.

As a husband, you can only lead your family as you are led by Christ. You can't do that if you're coasting on memories of your relationship with God. Jesus couldn't live without the Father, how can we expect to survive without him? Learn the way into the wild by following Jesus there. Then, lead your wife by giving her time to do the same.

Your bride also needs daily refreshment. And, if your wife is at all like mine (especially if you have children), she doesn't often feel the freedom or have time to escape to the wilderness. As her husband, it's part of your job to push her lovingly into the wild—to the secluded places where she can meet with and be refreshed by God. If she's not met with God recently, she likely feels tired, depleted, and dry. You can bless her by helping her find wilderness—by showing her to the trailhead that leads to an encounter with God. Sometimes the best way to pursue your bride is to stay behind and watch as God pursues her.

REFLECT

Do you regularly venture into the wild with the sole purpose of meeting with God? What are the most rewarding times you've spent alone?

How can your wife benefit from opportunities to spend time alone with God?

PRAY

Ask God to help you find time, intention, and opportunity for both of you to seek him.

Pursuit 6

ACT

⊘⊘⊘ | $ $ $

Give your wife the gift of time. Give her a "free pass" to spend two hours however she needs to most. No strings attached! Suggest she go for a walk, grab a coffee, read, or just spend some time in focused worship and prayer.

If you have kids, take them off her hands. Do whatever you can to pursue and serve her by giving her the time she needs to venture "into the wild."

___ *Check here when you've completed this pursuit.*

FIELD NOTES

Thoughts, feelings, or observations about today's pursuit?

She deserves this & needs to spend time w/ her friends

HEADS-UP!

Tomorrow's pursuit involves giving her a gift. You may want to make time to go shopping or make something.

7

The Generosity
of Love

*His divine power has granted to us all things that pertain to life
and godliness, through the knowledge of him who called us to his
own glory and excellence.*

2 PETER 1:3

*One gives freely, yet grows all the richer; another withholds what
he should give, and only suffers want. Whoever brings blessing
will be enriched, and one who waters will himself be watered.*

PROVERBS 11:24–25

The most famous verse in the Bible by far is John 3:16, and it's
popular for good reason. No other passage summarizes the core
of the Christian faith quite like it does in one succinct sentence.
The downside of knowing John 3:16 so well is that we can grow
numb to its powerful, transformational truth. We stop hearing
the depth and power behind it. If you aren't familiar with the

verse, I'm almost envious of you; I'd love to read it with fresh eyes. If you do know it well, try to read it slowly this time:

> *For God so loved the world, that he gave his only Son, that whoever believes in him should not perish but have eternal life.*

Catch that? God loved, so he gave. Giving is a natural—even inevitable—result of loving someone. Loving always leads to giving. Always. This single understanding forever changes how we view God, and, in turn, how we view our wives.

God's loving generosity also gives us magnificent context for the other verses we read in today's Scriptures. Peter wrote in 2 Peter 1:3 that God has "granted us all things that pertain to life and godliness." In Proverbs 11:24–25, Solomon reminds readers that generosity begets generosity, and stinginess brings more stinginess. As we read those passages with the knowledge that God gave to humanity because of his nature—his character of love—we see the radical, love-fueled generosity of God.

But his generosity is not without reason. God gave so he could get. He knew that his glad giving of himself (and "all things that pertain to life and godliness") would result in our glad giving of our own lives to him in worship, affection, and service. He gave to get his people—*us*—in return: our lives, our adoration, and our worship for eternity. In Christ, God pursued you to the death—giving his life—because that's *who* God is and that's *what* love does. That's the kind of pursuit we want to mirror—especially as husbands called to love our wives as Christ loved the church (Ephesians 5:25).

The early stages of a romantic relationship provide potent examples of generous love in action. Think back to when you and your wife first met. When you and her were just getting to know each other, you likely gave incredible amounts of time, energy, and even money to express your love. Long conversations, extravagant gifts, and elaborate thoughtfulness are all natural outpourings of affection—of love. This week we will focus on one of those expressions of thoughtfulness—gift giving—and put it into action in our pursuit of our wives.

When Selena and I started dating, it felt too good to be true. I was over-the-moon in love with her and wanted to show it to her at every opportunity. Our relationship was new, and every experience we shared was vivid and unforgettable. We'd dream and talk late into the night, and going home every evening was excruciating. I'd labor in thought over what gifts to buy her for special occasions; I'd even buy her random gifts just to show her I was thinking of her.

Now, recall your early relationship once more. Did you exchange gifts more than you do now? If so, what changed? Studying God's generous love reminds me of the power of giving to my wife. I'm reminded that when I give with a heart motivated by my love for her, it multiplies our affection and creates a culture of mutual generosity. That's why today's pursuit is about giving a gift; it's your opportunity to reflect God's generous love toward your wife in a tangible, obvious way.

REFLECT

How have you experienced God's love through his generosity? How has he blessed you? List at least three tangible ways.

How can God's generous love compel you to be intentionally more generous to your wife?

PRAY

Ask God for a deep understanding of his generous love, and clear conviction for ways you can love your wife generously as a result.

Pursuit 7

ACT   ⊙⊙⊙ | $$$

Give your wife an unexpected gift today. It doesn't have
to be expensive, but it should definitely be thoughtful.
In fact, feel free to go overboard with thoughtfulness!
That's where generosity is most felt. Wrap the gift and
include a handwritten note or card. When you present it
to her, explain to her that it's an expression of your love
and how you're committed to loving her generously for
the rest of your lives.

____ *Check here when you've completed this pursuit.*

FIELD NOTES

Thoughts, feelings, or observations about today's pursuit?

HEADS-UP!

Tomorrow's pursuit requires some dedicated time *for intimacy.*
Make sure your schedules allow at least two hours alone.

Let your fountain be blessed, and rejoice in the wife of your youth.

KING SOLOMON

DAY

8

An Intimate Pursuit

Drink water from your own cistern,
flowing water from your own well.
Should your springs be scattered abroad,
streams of water in the streets?
Let them be for yourself alone,
and not for strangers with you.
Let your fountain be blessed,
and rejoice in the wife of your youth,
a lovely deer, a graceful doe.
Let her breasts fill you at all times with delight;
be intoxicated always in her love.

PROVERBS 5:15–19

The Bible is not shy about sex. Nor does Scripture make light of it. Culture, however, seems confused. Just a few decades ago, sex was taboo—especially in the church. Now, it seems like everyone is talking about it. My whole perspective of sex changed when I learned God's view and purposes for it.

Sex is not taboo, but it *is* sacred. It's also good and healthy, but only within the right context. Sex can even be playful, but it's never flippant.

Sex is a physical expression of a spiritual commitment to loving the whole person. When you're naked with your wife, it's a beautiful representation of unity and intimacy that should exist in every level of your lives. Today's reading offers a remarkable picture of enjoying sex within marriage. Solomon compels readers to, "drink water from your own cistern" and "let them be for yourself alone." He even goes so far as to instruct husbands to "be intoxicated always in her love." That's strong language!

Most men desire sex more than their wives (though that's not always the case). That can mean that the wife sometimes feels steamrolled in the bedroom, or even pressured into having sex. I'll use myself as the example. My wife wants to be desired sexually, but not primarily or exclusively in that way. Since it would be unhelpful and perhaps unwise for me to assume I know how the sex dynamic works in your marriage, let's explore two universal truths about sex that apply no matter the situation.

First, sex is always exclusive. When Solomon instructs us to "drink water from your own cistern," he is saying, "enjoy what is yours and yours alone." It's isolated to you, your wife, and your marriage. Nothing from the outside should invade or contaminate your sexual experience, and your desire should be for your bride—for all of her—not just what she can do for you. The goal of sexual pursuit is not just physical pleasure, but rather a deeper bond—a mutual experience of complete, unhindered, and uncontaminated intimacy. A big part of keeping sex exclusive involves leaving all expectations, agendas, and preestablished ideas at the door. This frees you and your wife to focus on the same goal: each other. Again, sex is not about what your wife can do for you; it's about *who* she is to you.

Second, sex requires intentional communication. Selena and I have established (through many misfires and arguments) what we call the "Spectrum of Sex." It's basically the idea that not all sexual experiences have to be the same. Sex on one end of the spectrum is passionate and intense, and on the other end it's fast and functional. Both formats are edifying, just as long as you're on the same page. Having an agreed-upon spectrum of what sex can be like for us helps us avoid missed expectations and their resulting arguments. If we each have a similar idea of what to expect, we can be in agreement, experience unity, and grow in intimacy regardless of what the *act* of sex entails.

For today's pursuit, you are tasked with setting the stage and pursuing intimacy with your wife. Be advised, this could get tricky. Consider: How can you pursue your wife sexually while making certain she doesn't feel like she's a means to an end? You'll need to make sure you communicate extra carefully and sensitively. How does your wife feel most satisfied (on every level: emotionally, spiritually, physically) before, during, and after sex? As a husband, you know your wife better than anyone. It's your time to shine! Remember that *she* is your only goal. "Rejoice in the wife of your youth," and when in doubt, communicate. My prayer for you is that "your fountain be blessed," and your wife feels pursued, desired, and loved in endearing, honoring ways.

REFLECT

How can God be most glorified through your sex life as a married couple?

What makes your wife feel most desired? How does knowing that help you pursue her more purely?

PRAY

Ask God to bless your intimate life, and for health, healing, and growth in your sex life together. Seek wisdom from God in how to most edify your wife through how you pursue her sexually.

ACT   ☉☉☉ | $ $ $

Initiate intimacy with your wife in a way that she will feel most loved, honored, and pursued for *who* she is to you. Set the stage for romance in ways your wife will feel loved and safe. Consider romantic music, candles, and extravagant displays of romance (ex. rose petals trailing toward the bedroom).

Make sure to preface all romance with communication. Explain to your wife how and why you desire her for *who* she is, not just what she can do for you.

(If your bride is going through the wife's 31-Day Pursuit Challenge on the same schedule, she'll be reading about this topic as well.)

____ *Check here when you've completed this pursuit.*

FIELD NOTES

Thoughts, feelings, or observations about today's pursuit?

DAY

9

Honesty Is
Intimacy

*Confess your sins to one another and pray for one another, that
you may be healed. The prayer of a righteous person has great
power as it is working.*

JAMES 5:16

Nobody is perfect. Everyone understands this, but it's rarely a part of active conversation. And that's reasonable; no one likes to talk about their mistakes. But for those in the Christian faith, human imperfection is where the gospel begins. Acknowledging and confessing our own sin is the first step toward reconciliation with God. In it, we see ourselves as God sees us without Christ's intervention. We can then see clearly just how dramatically we fail to satisfy the requirements of righteousness and salvation. Sin may be the beginning of the gospel, but it's certainly not its end! While our sin exposes our raw need for a Savior, Jesus proves God's goodness and grace despite our sin! "God shows his love for us in that while we were still sinners, Christ died for us" (Romans 5:8).

Perhaps the most compelling truth of the gospel is that you are fully known to a completely holy God and still—*still*—you are loved. Doesn't that sound a lot like marriage? You know each other better than anyone, you're vulnerable and exposed on every level, and still you've vowed to love your spouse through everything, forsaking all others.

But God does not just save us from the fire and end the story there. He lovingly sanctifies us—makes us holy—until the day we die. Timothy Keller once said, "God invites us to come as we are, not to stay as we are."[2] Why else does James instruct believers to confess their sins? Surely he's not just providing talking points to alleviate awkward silences during small group gatherings. Confessing sin sanctifies our hearts and reconciles us to those around us (among other things).

Marriage offers an unparalleled arena for honesty, transparency, and therefore, love between two imperfect people. Here's how this played out for us. Early on in our marriage I realized that pornography was a constant source of temptation for me. Now I struggle with different sins, like worrying (not trusting God), wanting control (again, not trusting God), and impatience, to name a few. I only experienced freedom from sin when I confessed them to God and to Selena. Lasting freedom only began when I stopped fighting alone. Namely, I asked Selena for help and started living with full, unfiltered transparency. Confession of our sins to each other has become a constant rhythm in our marriage. I've given her permission to ask me anything, and in return I promised her (and myself) that I'd never lie, no matter how hard the truth is. I'll often schedule times to talk with her to divulge areas where the Holy Spirit is convicting me. I'll say something like, "Can we talk later tonight? I have something I need to share with you." When the time comes, we're both more ready for an intentional conversation, where emotions are under control and we can both prepare our hearts in advance by praying before we talk.

One remarkable outcome of my transparency with Selena is that she now feels more freedom to be transparent with me. Confessing our imperfections and sin to each other is never easy, but God is faithful to use us both in his sanctifying work in our individual hearts. As a result, our marriage flourishes as our understanding of the gospel deepens. Our love for each other grows as our affections for Jesus are stirred and amplified.

As a husband, you can lead your wife by confessing your own sin with confidence in Christ. She knows you're not perfect! If she doesn't know it yet, just give it time. There is too much at stake in life and marriage to let sin linger unconfessed. Not only that, but the rewards of living honestly with your wife are unsurpassed.

A NOTE ON GRACE

It's important to note that God's grace covers our sin for salvation, but the earthly consequences of our choices still remain.

For example, if you have unconfessed sexual sin (lust, pornography addiction, an affair), there will be consequences. That isn't to say that you can't work through anything with Jesus, but rather that it will take time to rebuild trust and reconcile your relationship.

Use wisdom in how and when you confess sin, but certainly do not delay. While the reconciliation process might look daunting, the alternative is much, *much* worse. Pursuing your bride through confession means that you're devoted to loving her through it, being patient while she heals, and seeking whatever help (pastoral care, counseling) necessary to reconcile your relationship.

REFLECT

What are three main benefits of transparent honesty in marriage?

- Trust
- open Communication
- builds a healthy Relationship

Are there areas where you can be more transparent with your wife? If so, what steps can you take to start an honest conversation?

When ask whats wrong

PRAY

Ask the Holy Spirit to reveal areas in your heart that need to be surrendered and confessed. Ask God to help you be brave and honest with telling your wife.

ACT   ☺☺☺ ⎸ $ $ $

Make a date with your wife to share what you learned from today's reading, reflection questions, and prayer. Preface your conversation by explaining why you value transparency with her and want to pursue her by being completely honest in light of the gospel.

Depending on where you're at, this might be *very* hard. Move forward with confidence in Christ; trust him to be faithful.

___ *Check here when you've completed this pursuit.*

FIELD NOTES

Thoughts, feelings, or observations about today's pursuit?

DAY

10

Extravagant Encouragement

Anxiety in a man's heart weighs him down,
but a good word makes him glad.

PROVERBS 12:25

Without counsel plans fail,
but with many advisers they succeed.
To make an apt answer is a joy to a man,
and a word in season, how good it is!

PROVERBS 15:22–23

Words are powerful avenues for encouragement, but the best encouragement goes far beyond words alone. Think back to a time when you felt most encouraged. Why do you suppose you felt that way? It was likely because you felt particularly anxious or weighed down, and someone came alongside you in that moment and gave you "a word in season." When you heard their words, they put your soul to rest and infused your heart with fresh courage. The most powerful encouragement always comes at a time when it's desperately needed, from someone who knows you and your circumstance.

Here's how that plays out in my marriage dynamic. I've always had an entrepreneurial bug. When Selena and I finally decided to step out and start our first business, things weren't easy. We moved fifteen hundred miles away from home, had very little, and the economy was just starting a severe downswing (this was mid-2008). There were countless opportunities for doubt and worry—which I readily took advantage of. But Selena was always strong in my weak moments. As my wife, she has unique access to my heart. In those hard times, she could have doubted with me, but instead she encouraged me to keep going. She reminded me of God's sovereign, perfect provision amid our apparent lack. She infused me with faith, confidence, energy, and courage to carry on. Oh, how grateful I am for my wife's timely encouragements! Without her "words in season," I would have surely quit. Instead, we fought through the hard times together and grew stronger as a couple in the process.

For me, one of the most important markers of effective encouragement is context. In both of today's passages, we see the context—or a mutually understood circumstance—for both the giver and the receiver of words of encouragement. In the first case, "a man's heart weighs him down" and in the second, a specific issue is being considered and addressed. This is why spouses have such a unique ability to speak into each others' hearts; no one on earth knows you and your circumstances or has a greater stake in your life than your wife.

Another word that describes encouragement is *heartening*. Apt encouragement bolsters—props up, strengthens, and reinforces—the heart. Jesus heartens us by reminding us of his divine role as Savior and King. He says, "Come to me, all who labor and are heavy laden, and I will give you rest" (Matthew 11:28). He promises a "Helper, to be with you forever" (John 14:16), otherworldly peace (John 14:27), and so much more. His words always bolster the hearts of believers, but the key to receiving his encouragement is *context*—it's trust. Christ knows your context better than you do, but do you trust him? Do you desire his "words in season"? If you do, you will have them. If you don't trust or desire Jesus, his encouragements will fall on deaf ears and a hardened heart. Still, he will never stop heartening his sheep regardless of how well they (we) respond.

Encouragement always says more about the encourager than the one encouraged. Just as Christ has encouraged you, you are called to encourage your bride. But truly encouraging words always take into account the other's circumstance, need, and language. Every "apt answer" is appropriate for the question—the need—being addressed.

As a husband, you have a unique ability to encourage your wife. Think about her context and how you can provide a "good word." Think about how Christ encourages his followers. Think about how you're personally encouraged by Christ. Let your experience being encouraged by Christ fuel how you pursue your bride through your timely, apt words of encouragement. As a husband loving your bride as Christ loved the church, you are equipped for the role in her life only you can fill. Use your access to her heart to strengthen it and remind her of the God you serve, his promises, and her identity in him.

REFLECT

What is one time when God's words have encouraged you in a severe time of need? Why do you think they were especially encouraging in that moment?

Now, think about times when your wife has best reacted to encouragement from you. What about your encouragement spoke to her most?

PRAY

Ask God for insight into ways your wife can be encouraged, and for sureness of God's grace in both of your hearts.

Pursuit 10

ACT   ◔◕◑ | $ $ $

Think about the following questions:

1.) Lately, how have I been stewarding this "direct access" to my wife's heart?

2.) What challenges is she facing that require courage?

3.) How can I encourage and help strengthen her?

4.) What timely words will speak most to her?

Consider ways your words (as her husband) can infuse her with confidence. Text her (or give her a note) with these three things: a few timely words of encouragement, a prayer over her, and one verse meant to strengthen her.

____ *Check here when you've completed this pursuit.*

FIELD NOTES

Thoughts, feelings, or observations about today's pursuit?

11

Authentic Empathy

He had to be made like his brothers in every respect, so that he might become a merciful and faithful high priest in the service of God, to make propitiation for the sins of the people. For because he himself has suffered when tempted, he is able to help those who are being tempted.

HEBREWS 2:17–18

So much of building a thriving marriage requires communication. But the core purpose of communication isn't just to say more words. It's to truly understand each other, find agreement, maintain unity, and empathize with one another. The most effective communication happens when both of you are able to hear what the other person is saying, while also being heard yourself. But if we look a bit further, we find that the motivations for hearing and being heard are what actually matter to a healthy marriage: genuine empathy, unity, softness of heart, and closeness.

Selena is a stay-at-home mom whose work is eternal. She works harder than anyone I know. Truly. I know you could probably say the same thing about your wife. She sleeps less, accomplishes more, and cares for more human lives for longer hours than I ever could. Who she is and what she does for our family are irreplaceable. I'd also say that my roles and responsibilities as husband and dad are also irreplaceable for our family. Could either one of us take over the other person's duties? Perhaps in some ways, but I'd rather not find out. We're pretty good at appreciating each other, but we definitely lose sight of each other's value at times. The vast majority of our arguments happen because we've failed to understand each other and extend grace as a result.

Six months after our second daughter was born, I received a crash course in Selena's job. It wasn't pretty, but I learned a ton. We received a phone call one Saturday morning at 6:30 a.m. Selena's grandma, who had been fighting a blood infection, had taken a turn for the worse. Her doctors estimated that she'd pass away within a few hours, so everyone in the family decided to rally together to spend those last moments with her and say their good-byes. Selena was out the door less than ten minutes after receiving the call and—neither of us knew this—wouldn't return home for twelve hours. I faintly heard something about giving plenty of food and water to the baby (or was it the dogs?) as the door closed behind her. Suddenly, there I was, alone with two wonderful pairs of little-girl eyes staring up at me. I felt unprepared, but it was not the time to be needy; Selena needed my help, and I wasn't about to buckle under the pressure!

Grandma went to be with Jesus, and Selena had the beautiful privilege of being there until the very end. She was thankful, and so was I! But I was also exhausted, even with the help of my gracious parents. I had experienced (to a lesser degree) what Selena does every single day, and it forever changed how I appreciate her. I could finally *empathize*.

How many times could I have understood her sooner if I had empathized more completely? How many arguments could have been avoided? It was a light-bulb moment for me in our marriage. Someone once said, "You don't know what you don't know." I see new merit in that statement. I'm now much quicker to try and understand my wife's perspective than I am to argue mine.

Thank God for a Savior who can empathize with our weakness! As today's passage says, Jesus "had to be made like his brothers in every respect, so that he might become a merciful and faithful high priest in the service of God." Your struggles are not foreign to Jesus. You're not alone in your temptation, and you're covered by grace in your failure. We do not serve a King who fails to empathize with our needs, our temptations, or our humanity. Jesus pursued you, became flesh, died a human death, and conquered death on your behalf—all by the good grace of God! How much more can we pursue our wives by learning to empathize with their day-to-day lives?

As a husband, let it be your primary charge to understand your wife more each day. An author once wrote, "It takes two years to learn to speak and sixty to learn to keep quiet." Put your words on pause and just listen. Listen to your bride, hear what she's saying, and seek understanding. Put yourself in her shoes every chance you get! Your empathy will only help your marriage and bless your wife. As I learned, you truly don't know what you don't know, and what you discover will likely surprise you!

REFLECT

In what ways do you find it hard to empathize with your wife?

How can you learn to better empathize with her in those areas?

PRAY

Ask God to increase your empathy and patience with your wife.

Pursuit 11

ACT

⏱ ⏱ ⏱ | $ $ $

Pursue your wife by taking a routine responsibility off her plate. The task can be big or small, and it might take ten minutes or two hours—your call. Whatever you do, make sure she feels relieved by not having to do it. While you're "relieving her," seek to understand her perspective just a little more.

Afterward, take a moment to express your appreciation for everything she does to contribute to your household.

___ *Check here when you've completed this pursuit.*

FIELD NOTES

Thoughts, feelings, or observations about today's pursuit?

HEADS-UP!

Tomorrow you will need at least thirty minutes to talk *vision*. Make sure you and your wife both have ample time.

DAY

12

Partnering in Vision and Faith

And the LORD answered me:
"Write the vision;
make it plain on tablets,
so he may run who reads it.
For still the vision awaits its appointed time;
it hastens to the end—it will not lie.
If it seems slow, wait for it;
it will surely come; it will not delay."

HABAKKUK 2:2–3

God-given desires are good and worthy pursuits. They will never trump your highest call to desire God most, but God does not give his people visions in vain. Of course, as believers, we must guard our hearts against the subtle idolatry of seeking ultimate satisfaction through fulfilling our own desires, but when we want something and place our trust in God to satisfy us, he will never disappoint. We need only stay the course and trust in his divine plan more than our own. Even if his plans differ from our own, we will always find satisfaction when we look for it in him.

Today's reading is from the book of Habakkuk, which was written during a time when Israel and Judah (God's people) were suffering at the hands of their enemies. The theme of the book is about questioning God's methods (for allowing his people to be conquered) and ultimately resting in his sovereignty. The author questioned God (1:2), then God responded by telling the author to trust him (1:5). Eventually Habakkuk gave up control and put his faith in God (3:18). It's a remarkable, short book—one definitely worth reading (or rereading) when you get the chance.

Today's verses are God's response to Habakkuk's second complaint. God instructed him to write down what he said clearly so the people of God could read it and remember to trust him. Matthew Henry, an eighteenth-century minister, eloquently expanded on the passage's meaning:

> *When tossed and perplexed with doubts about the methods of Providence, we must watch against temptations to be impatient. When we have poured out complaints and requests before God, we must observe the answers God gives by his word, his Spirit, and providences; what the Lord will say to our case. God will not disappoint the believing expectations of those who wait to hear what he will say unto them.*[3]

Much of the Christian walk entails asking God hard questions, observing his answers in his Word, and trusting him with the parts we don't understand. That's faith, and it's the life-attitude to which we're called as followers of Christ.

What a liberating blessing it is to read Scriptures like these and see how God kept his word! In the New Testament, Paul quoted the words of Habakkuk when he taught on faith-fueled righteousness in Christ (Romans 1:17, Galatians 3:11). You and I can read about the coming of Jesus as fulfillment of God's promise to redeem his people. Today, we have the privilege of observing God's faithfulness in the past, but Habakkuk and Judah did not. That is precisely why God told Habakkuk to write the vision down and make it plain to read: to remind God's people to trust him, especially when it was hardest. Yet, despite our access to the Bible, we still need to be reminded of God's promises daily.

What hard questions are you asking God that seem unanswered? What hard questions is your wife wrestling with? How is the Holy Spirit spurring you with vision that requires you to trust God more completely? How are you expecting God to move in your lives as a result?

Day-to-day life doesn't readily offer opportunities to discuss God's vision and purpose for your lives with your spouse. And sometimes life's demands (a mortgage payment, job security, general busyness) can choke the faith out of daily living. Today's challenge is to lead your bride in a conversation about God's vision for your lives. Specifically, how is God calling her to step out in faith and trust him more? As a husband you are called to serve your wife with reckless abandon while leading her with gentleness, wisdom, and discernment. The most loving thing you can do for her is to urge her toward a more radical faith in Jesus. It's time to explore God's vision in your wife's life—her God-given talents, dreams, and goals—and look for ways to support her in faithfully pursuing them for God's ultimate glory.

REFLECT

Do you have a strong vision for how God is calling you and your wife? If so, what is it? If not, how do you think he's calling you?

How is God calling your wife individually? How can you better encourage your wife in her strengths and giftings?

PRAY

Ask God for vision and the ability to hear his voice and leading.

ACT   ⏱⏱⏱ | $ $ $

Before you go to bed tonight, spend at least thirty minutes with your wife discussing her purpose and dreams. Ask her to articulate what she's passionate about and how she feels called to serve Jesus with her time, talent, and treasure. Explore ways that you can come alongside her through prayer, actions, and encouragement.

Whatever you discuss, write it down! If possible, create a tangible plan to begin stepping out in faith as the Holy Spirit prompts.

Consider ordering takeout to help minimize dinner prep or cleanup required of either of you.

____ *Check here when you've completed this pursuit.*

FIELD NOTES

Thoughts, feelings, or observations about today's pursuit?

13

Serving Is Pursuing

When he had washed their feet and put on his outer garments
and resumed his place, he said to them, "Do you understand
what I have done to you? You call me Teacher and Lord, and
you are right, for so I am. If I then, your Lord and Teacher, have
washed your feet, you also ought to wash one another's feet. For I
have given you an example, that you also should do
just as I have done to you.

JOHN 13:12–15

The scene of Jesus washing his disciples' feet is astounding. At first glance, we rightly assume that Jesus was simply calling his followers to serve others. That was clearly part of his intent, but there's much more! There are at least three key truths we can learn from Jesus' washing of the disciples' feet. And as we'll see, they offer incredible implications for how you can pursue your bride.

The first truth we see is that Jesus' actions foreshadowed

his ultimate act of servanthood through death on the cross. In ancient culture, feet were generally filthy and particularly exposed during meals as people reclined at low tables. The washing of feet before meals was customary. John was very intentional in describing how Jesus prepared to wash his disciple's feet: "He laid aside his outer garments, and taking a towel, tied it around his waist" (John 13:4). He then used that towel to wipe their feet dry after washing. Why did John include this part about the towel? Wouldn't readers just assume he'd have a towel? Apparently there was more to it. It could be true that Jesus' removal of his outer garment (his robe or mantle) and attaching the towel signified the removal of his divine mantle (his role in heaven) and donning of humanity for the work to come on the cross. Jesus took on the sin of the world, and he covers believers with his righteousness, much like he dirtied the towel with their foot-filth and covered it with his outer garment once again. (John never mentions him removing the towel.)

Second, Jesus was countering the proud attitudes of the disciples. In Luke's parallel account, the disciples were caught fighting over who would be regarded as the greatest (22:24). Jesus' example of humility and servanthood would have shocked them. How could he, their Teacher, stoop to such a level? Jesus used his own example to remind them that "the leader is one who serves" (v. 26). In God's economy, the greatest are the least, the richest are the poorest, and the last shall be first. He was discrediting their proud attitudes and refocusing them on what matters most to God.

Third, Jesus reminded his disciples to follow his example by serving each other. As they sat down to eat, there were no servants in sight who could wash their feet. Yet, it didn't occur to any of them to step in and serve their brothers in that way. As I mentioned, washing feet wasn't a formality or a nicety; it was a required prerequisite to a sanitary meal! To refuse to wash each other's feet would have been to say, "I'd rather not eat than do that!" There's a good chance the notion of washing the others' feet occurred to one of them, but as we see, no one acted on it. Jesus' example is a potent reminder that we're called to get our hands dirty by serving others, and we shouldn't allow pride or forgetfulness to get in the way.

I'm sure you're starting to see the parallels of how you can pursue your wife by serving her in all three ways we've explored. As her husband, you can model *Christ on the cross* by giving of yourself freely, selflessly, and sacrificially. You can exemplify Jesus' *servant leadership* by guiding your wife gently with her best interests in mind. Finally, you can tangibly serve her by *assuming a servant's role* in your household; you can take it upon yourself to actively look for ways to alleviate her burdens and meet her needs.

To us the act of washing feet is generally symbolic, but it's vivid. Shocking, even. Just as Jesus' example caught his disciples by surprise, you're likely to shock your wife when you begin actively pursuing her—leading her—through service.

REFLECT

Think of one time in the past when you've been served radically and unexpectedly. How did it make you feel? What effect did it have on your heart, attitude, and appreciation?

What are three ways you can better serve your wife?

PRAY

Ask God for an increased heart of servanthood.

Pursuit 13

ACT

⊙⊙⊙ | $ $ $

This evening, take the time to wash your wife's feet. Have her sit in a comfortable chair, grab a bowl, some water, and a towel. Explain Jesus' example of servant leadership to his bride—the church—and how you're learning to pursue her in the same way.

If you feel led, read John 13:1–17 out loud and pray with her. Either way, just serve her and keep it light-hearted.

(If your wife is going through her 31-Day Pursuit Challenge on the same schedule, she'll have the same pursuit for the day.)

____ *Check here when you've completed this pursuit.*

FIELD NOTES

Thoughts, feelings, or observations about today's pursuit?

HEADS-UP!

In two days you'll be tasked with preparing dinner for a special date at home. You may want to glance ahead and start planning!

DAY

14

The Gift of Gladness

Greet one another with the kiss of love.

1 Peter 5:14

Welcome one another as Christ has welcomed you,
for the glory of God.

Romans 15:7

Selena and I spent some time in Switzerland after college, chasing dreams and working odd jobs. One of my most vivid memories is of one time when we were at the Zürich train station grabbing a bite to eat in what might be considered a food court, with different restaurants and vendors offering a variety of food and wares. One of the places sold amazing döner kebabs (gyro-wrap-things) that were incredibly fresh and always delicious. They were so good, in fact, that we decided to return after having been there multiple times before. Having spent the day on foot, we were both especially hungry. We each ordered our usual. It took a few minutes, but our food finally arrived and we dove right in. As we ate and conversed, everything seemed normal, until . . .

I was about three bites in and going in for a fourth. As I looked at my food to line up my next approach, my eyes were met with a horrific sight. Without thinking, I did what any red-blooded human would do: I violently spewed the contents of my mouth all over my wife, the table, and the floor.

It was like the world transitioned to slow motion. Selena's eyes widened with shock and terror as she dove for cover. Lettuce, tomatoes, chunks of lamb, and various condiments shot out of my mouth and nose like culinary shrapnel. The shop owner was petrified.

"What in the world are you doing!?" Selena shouted. She may have used slightly more colorful language; it's all a blur . . .

After a few moments, we recovered and I showed her the problem. Tucked neatly inside my döner kebab, there was a huge, white, squirming larva of some sort. As it turns out, the lettuce they used was *so* fresh that it was still home to this translucent abomination. This thing, whatever it was, was actually quite harmless. Still, that doesn't mean I want it in my food.

I composed myself and showed the shop owner our buggy discovery. She asked if I wanted a refund or new food. I politely opted for the refund. My appetite had vanished.

Fun story, but what's the point? Small things can easily contaminate otherwise delightful experiences. Conversely, small things can also make a huge positive difference in a negative situation. Have you ever come home from a great day only to find that your wife is in a bad mood, irritated with you, or indifferent to your arrival? If so, you understand how a small negative moment can reverse an entire day of positivity. How many times have *you* been the downer?

Today's passage includes a portion of Peter's closing remarks to readers in the early church. They were distraught from persecution, and much of his first letter was written to strengthen and encourage them to endure trials with faithfulness and joy. He ended his exhortations with, "Greet one another with a kiss of love." In the first century, a "kiss of love," otherwise called a "kiss of charity," was a common method of affectionately greeting brothers in Christ. It's like throwing a mini celebration every time you greet a friend. You can feel Peter's affection for his brothers and sisters as you read his words. The weight of their persecution was not lost on him, yet he urged them to celebrate each other with intentionally affectionate greetings.

If you've been married for a while, you understand that it's not all fresh lettuce and delicious lamb meat. (I bet you've never heard it said like that before.) Sometimes "contaminants" sneak in, and it feels as if everything has been ruined. There are also times of sustained struggle when you feel tired and worn out, much like the members of the early church felt. Especially in those times, a "kiss of love"—an enthusiastic, affectionate greeting—is exactly what you need to remind yourselves that you're on the same side, you share the same goal, and your unwavering hope is in Christ.

Many times, the "worm" in your marriage is just plain familiarity and forgetfulness. Don't let small contaminants rob your wife of those "kiss of love" moments. Greet her with all the genuine gladness and joy warranted you through the gospel. "Rejoice in the wife of your youth" (Proverbs 5:18). Pursue her with fresh eyes each day and greet her with gladness every chance you get. Even the smallest gestures of gospel-fueled love will have a profound impact on your marriage.

REFLECT

How do you greet your wife after not seeing her for a few hours or more? How can you improve?

PRAY

Ask God to fill you with a new spirit of gladness. Pray for mutual joy in your marriage.

ACT

🕐🕑🕒 | $ $ $

Today's challenge isn't as much a one-time thing as it is the beginning of a new habit (or refreshing an old one). The next time you see your wife, greet her with genuine, glad affection. You decide what that means to you; just be sure to celebrate her! It could be a kiss, a hug, a smile, or affectionate words.

___ *Check here when you've completed this pursuit.*

FIELD NOTES

Thoughts, feelings, or observations about today's pursuit?

HEADS-UP!

Are you ready for tomorrow's dinner date? You got this.

Happy is the man who finds a true friend, and far happier is he who finds that true friend in his wife.

FRANZ SCHUBERT

15

Breaking Bread, Breaking Routine

Day by day, attending the temple together and breaking bread in their homes, they received their food with glad and generous hearts, praising God and having favor with all the people.

ACTS 2:46–47

The book of Acts shows us the beginning of the early church. We get to witness the first stages of the world-changing culture shock that began after Jesus rose from the grave and ascended to heaven. The entire world was turned upside down. Imagine what that must have been like! Jesus satisfied the requirements of the old covenant (justification through law-keeping) and ushered all of humanity into a new era of justification through faith and grace. The impact of such a transition cannot be overstated. These men and women who had lived their entire lives as slaves under the law were suddenly and absolutely *free* because of Jesus Christ. What joy and relief they must have felt!

Today's passage provides a glimpse of exactly how the early church celebrated. They attended temple gatherings and ate meals together as a faith community, all with glad, generous, and worshipful hearts. They had every reason for joy. Up until then they had been under the law; but suddenly they were free! I imagine they felt an amplified version of what I feel after tax day.

Jesus' pursuit of us spans from the Garden of Eden to the cross and beyond. Every covenant God made with his people points to his ultimate end of reconciling us to him through Christ. What we read in the book of Acts is the aftermath of Christ's resurrection as fulfillment of those early covenants. What it must have been like to be alive in those days! To feel so nearly and tangibly the outpouring of fresh, new grace.

Christianity as we know it today is the result of the early church fulfilling their call to spread the gospel throughout Judea, Samaria, and the Mediterranean. If you've heard the good news of grace through Jesus, it's because of the work God began in Acts.

As a result, you and I can participate in the celebration! Though we won't ever truly understand the burden early Christians felt under the law or their relief when it was fulfilled, we can experience the radical freedom of Christ as sinners saved by grace. In that freedom, we can live with the same extraordinary joy. Because of Christ, every church gathering holds new meaning, every meal tastes richer, and every relationship now bears the mark of the gospel—especially your marriage.

Each day with your wife is a gift. *She* is a gift. It's easy to forget the magnitude of those facts. As a husband, never let yourself tire of appreciating your bride as a gracious blessing from God. Your wife is God's most obvious blessing in your life. So, what can you do to remind yourself and her of that truth?

Every celebration starts with gratitude. The key to celebrating your wife and valuing your marriage is gratefulness. In today's verses, we witness the glad results of receiving from God. Those in the early church were profoundly happy—not in their circumstances (because they were under heavy persecution), but in their newfound purpose and freedom in Christ.

In life and marriage your circumstances will shift constantly, but your purpose and freedom won't. That, my friend, is cause to celebrate! In fact, the entire Christian life is one of celebratory worship.

Continue your lifelong celebration by remembering the profound blessing your wife is. Tonight you'll be celebrating in the tradition of Christian joy over a special meal. Break bread with your bride with glad, generous, and worshipful hearts. As you do, you'll be walking in the same joy experienced by your brothers and sisters in Christ thousands of years ago.

REFLECT

Think back to a time in your life when you've celebrated with unbridled enthusiasm. Why was that occasion remarkable?

What are a few recent causes for celebration in your marriage?

How can you create a constant atmosphere of gratitude for all God is doing in your lives?

PRAY

Give thanks for the Christian tradition of joy! Ask God for new insight into how to make joy in him a part of your every meal.

Pursuit 15

ACT   ☺☺☺ | $$$

Plan an at-home date night. Consider cooking her something special. Light some candles and set the atmosphere; consider dressing nice for the occasion.

As you "break bread" together, celebrate your relationship; celebrate *her*. Celebrate God's grace! You may want to let her know what to expect in advance and how she can prepare (by wearing appropriate attire, or adjusting her schedule).

___ *Check here when you've completed this pursuit.*

FIELD NOTES

Thoughts, feelings, or observations about today's pursuit?

DAY

16

The Work of Love

Love is patient and kind.

1 CORINTHIANS 13:4

Recently I was in a gas station line waiting to pay the cashier. There were two guys in line ahead of me (we'll call them John and Tim). The guy at the counter (Tim) looked disheveled—like he had been walking for a long time with very little rest. He was young but weathered. Still, with bright eyes and a warm smile, Tim placed his items on the counter: Mountain Dew, beef jerky, and a bag of chips.

"Five eighty-three," totaled the cashier. I noticed a mild look of annoyance and suspicion in his eyes. This particular gas station gets a decent amount of transient foot traffic, so his concern likely stemmed from past experiences.

Agreeing to the amount, Tim dug into his pockets but came up empty. A look of embarrassment flooded his face. He pulled his backpack off before shuffling himself and his items off to the side. "I got it . . . just one second," he started. After a few seconds, it became clear that he was a little short for cash. The shop owner raised his eyebrows and opened his mouth to speak. I braced for an awkward experience.

"I'll get his stuff," John (the other guy) interrupted.

The cashier was bewildered, "You . . . you'll pay for his stuff?"

"Yeah, I got this," John confirmed.

The look on Tim's face was a mixture of shock and gratitude. "It's okay man, I can—" Tim started.

But John interrupted again, "No worries, brother, I got you."

Witnessing an act of kindness "in the wild" is rare. Whenever I do, I marvel at the obvious connection between kindness and the felt presence of love. As you read in the above verse, Paul plainly states, "Love is patient and kind." In Galatians, he connects kindness and love as fruits of the spirit (Galatians 5:22–23). The two are inextricable. Love without kindness is false love.

What is kindness, exactly? We can start to understand what makes kindness unique by contrasting it with patience. While both are aspects of love, Paul distinguished them for a reason. Patience is an inward reaction, whereas kindness tends to be an outward expression. I like to think of kindness as love with its sleeves rolled up—it's the *work of love*. Kindness is love that isn't afraid to get its hands dirty. It actively engages in the tasks of love by going out of its way to serve others, give freely, and acknowledge genuine affection.

It's impossible to be loving and unkind at the same time. Love and kindness are like water and wetness: one is the substance and the other, its evidence. A man driven by Spirit-filled love will exhibit increasing awareness and actions of proactive kindness.

Of course, the examples of Jesus' kindness in the Bible are vast, but how is he kind to you personally? If we consider it kindness for John to pay for Tim's snacks, how much more kind to us is Christ on the cross? You and I, who were once indebted to God beyond all hope and lost in sin, have been released from all debt! We were pursued and found by God himself. God is love (1 John 4:8), and he embodies the type of love that isn't afraid to get involved. God's sovereign pull—his drawing you near through Jesus—is the kindest, most active display of love imaginable. *We're all Tims.* We stand at eternity's counter with our pockets turned out until Jesus kindly interrupts, saying, "No worries, brother, I got you."

It's easy for husbands to be unintentionally unkind to their wives. I know that's the case for me. If I'm not careful, I can speak in ways that are mean, insensitive, and self-focused. I can be thoughtless and unaware of "I got you" opportunities. My wife isn't so fragile that I can break her, but she's delicate. She hears words in ways that I don't hear them. She feels in ways I don't feel. My inaction and silence can seem cold. If I'm to be kind to her, I must consider how my actions, words, inaction, and silence affect her. Are all husbands called to love their wives by walking on eggshells every hour of every day? Hardly. But it doesn't hurt to spare a few eggshells if it means pursuing your bride with love and kindness.

REFLECT

How has Christ shown you kindness? List three specific ways.

How can you show your wife more kindness through your words, actions, and responses?

PRAY

Ask God for insight into what actions of kindness will be most effective in showing love to your wife.

Pursuit 16

ACT

🕐🕐🕐 | $ $ $

Go out of your way to show your wife kindness today. Get creative. You could serve her, encourage her, give her a small gift, bring her lunch, or do whatever else comes to mind. Do whatever will speak to her most vividly.

The key is pursuing your bride by putting your hands to the "work of love" by showing her proactive kindness.

___ *Check here when you've completed this pursuit.*

FIELD NOTES

Thoughts, feelings, or observations about today's pursuit?

HEADS-UP!

You're over halfway through this book. Great job! Day 31 is about two weeks away. Have you decided what you're going to do?

DAY
17

Write Like a Warrior

Behold, you are beautiful, my love,
behold, you are beautiful!
Your eyes are doves
behind your veil.

SONG OF SOLOMON 4:1

The modern concept of manliness is a funny, fickle thing. It's in constant flux. Historically, manhood has always, to some extent, been defined by physical strength, bravery, and honor. Strength makes sense because, in general, men are larger and stronger than women. Bravery involves a man's willingness to face fear and peril for a high cause. You could say that bravery refers to a man's mental strength. Honor is the measure of a man's character and conviction, or his heart strength—his moral substance. Indeed, honor is the fuel behind every true feat of bravery. A brave man without honor you might find, but an honorable man without bravery you'll never find. Honor always produces bravery, but the reverse isn't necessarily true. Give me a weak man with honor over a strong man without honor every time.

Honor is about what or who a man cares for—it's about what lies on the *other side* of the battle. A man with honor will fight any enemy to protect and pursue those he cares about most. If ever he turns away, he reveals his true desire—himself and self-preservation—and thus, his honor is stripped away. Again, the single distinguishing mark of honor is what a man cares about.

It's not common nowadays to associate manliness with romantic literature, but let's change that. If what a man cares about determines his honor (a key aspect to manliness), then the effective expression of his passion for his wife, to his wife, is appropriately *manly*. This doesn't mean that every man need be an aspiring poet or Shakespeare wannabe. I'm living proof of that.

On our wedding day, I sang Selena a song I'd written for her. It was many things, but objectively good wasn't one of them. Every time Selena and I reminisce about that portion of our wedding ceremony, Selena always tells me how amazing it was . . . for *her*. I've played guitar since I was thirteen, and I started singing in formal settings (jazz ensemble, worship team) not too long after. I can now look back at my wedding-day serenade and say with near certainty that I absolutely butchered it. I was a nervous, sweaty, emotional mess. I forgot half of the second verse and compensated by mumbling a few inaudible words into the microphone. I cringe whenever we watch the video, but Selena cries. Why? Because she feels loved.

Romantic gestures need not be perfect to effectively communicate affection—they need only be genuine. Thank God!

I chose today's passage because of its stark contrast between the context of the moment and the character of Solomon. Just a few verses before he waxes poetic, Solomon entered the scene on a king's couch, carried and surrounded by sixty mighty warriors of Israel, "each with his sword at his thigh, against terror by night" (Song of Solomon 3:7–8). His entrance is a display of manliness, honor, royalty, and extravagance. Solomon was a leader of warriors, a man after God, and a wise ruler of God's people. He was undoubtedly manly, yet we have him to thank for most of the Bible's romantic language. Manliness and passionate words go hand in hand.

Communicating romantically can be intimidating, especially when you do it creatively. Writing, speaking, and singing with passion aren't skills many men develop by default. You may even discount your ability to express yourself romantically because you don't consider yourself especially gifted. Still, don't let that stop you! Today's pursuit is about communicating your passion romantically by putting pen to paper. Trust me, you can do it.

While some individuals are certainly gifted in singing, writing, and speaking, romantic communication is a skill that can be mastered. Even more importantly, passionately communicating your love for your bride, to your bride, is a skill that *only you* can master. No one knows your wife like you, and no one's genuine words of romantic adoration will affect her as deeply as yours.

REFLECT

What books, songs, poems, movies, or stories have left an impression on you in the past? Why were they especially moving?

What artistic expressions move your wife most? Music, literature, poetry? How can you apply what you know to how you pursue her both today and in the future?

PRAY

Ask God for divine creative inspiration in how you express your affection to your wife. If you find expressing yourself difficult, pray for vulnerability and faith to follow through with today's challenge even if you don't feel prepared.

ACT

⊙⊙⊙ | $ $ $

Pursue your wife by putting pen to paper. Write a poem, a song, or a letter that expresses your love and passion for your bride. If it doesn't come easy for you, keep trying! It's good to labor over romance. The objective isn't perfection; it's authenticity. It helps to remember that the point isn't to prove how skilled you are, but rather to communicate how much your wife means to you. When you're finished, share what you've written with her.

(If your wife is going through her own 31-Day Pursuit Challenge, she'll have to do this too. Show her how it's done!)

____ *Check here when you've completed this pursuit.*

FIELD NOTES

Thoughts, feelings, or observations about today's pursuit?

HEADS-UP!

In two days you will be doing something spontaneous. Depending on what you do, you may need to set aside time beforehand.

DAY
18

An Obvious Pursuit

He is able to save to the uttermost those who draw near to God through him, since he always lives to make intercession for them.

HEBREWS 7:25

I once read a statement by author Michael Hyatt that immediately embedded itself in my thinking as a husband. He said, "I will speak often and lovingly of my wife. (This is the best adultery repellent known to man.)"[4] What a simple, profound statement! Nothing publicly solidifies your commitment to your wife quite like speaking of her often with glowing affection.

Affairs rarely happen out of the blue; they start small and progress subtly over time. Every affair begins in the imagination, takes root in the heart, and slowly turns into action. Intentionally displaying and communicating your affection for your wife is an effective defense against thoughts, attitudes, and actions of infidelity.

Let me illustrate with a personal example. When we lived in Southern California, I worked out at a nearby gym. The woman who managed the front desk was attractive and sometimes flirtatious. I found myself tempted by the opportunity of being liked by an attractive woman (forgetting entirely that I was already deeply loved by the woman of my dreams—my wife). By God's grace I grew terrified of the situation—I foresaw impending disaster and realized no good could come of it. So the next time I saw the woman, I made it a point to talk about Selena casually but deliberately. I imagined my wife there with me. *What would she think if she were here?* The instant I referenced Selena by name and used the phrase "my wife" with genuine affection, the situation was defused. Thank God.

Making your pursuit of your wife obvious to others has at least three tangible effects. First, it stirs your affections for her and realigns your heart. Just the mere mention of your wife will reaffirm in your heart every good and true thing about your marriage.

Second, making your affections obvious causes your bride to feel loved, cherished, and honored. I've found it helpful to imagine Selena listening and/or watching me when I'm alone. I ask myself if she'd feel honored and loved if she witnessed my actions. It's not about being paranoid or prudish, but rather about defending my own heart against temptation. Then, when your wife is present or if she speaks with a colleague of yours and learns about how often you mention her, she will inevitably feel loved, honored, and cherished.

Finally, your obvious pursuit makes your devotion to your wife unquestionable to others. When you mention your wife (especially by name) or speak lovingly about her, you leave no room for doubt. When you include her by name, you bring her into the conversation and put all weirdness to rest. Your friends, coworkers, and acquaintances will respect you, your wife, and your marriage. Finally, those who would actively seek to divide your marriage will have nowhere to start chipping away at your foundation.

Does all this mean you must have a perfect marriage or at least act like you do? No. When you speak lovingly of your bride, you're not faking it, but quite the opposite. You're reminding yourself and others of one of the most potent truths in your life—you have committed to loving your wife exclusively and in increasing measure until the day you die! Every time you make your love for her known, you're reiterating the commitment you made on your wedding day.

You may be wondering what today's passage has to do with pursuing your bride obviously and in public. As the verse says, Jesus "always lives to make intercession" for those who draw near to him. Jesus is God's fulfillment of his promise to save his people—his covenant to send a Redeemer, a Savior, and a King. There is nothing Satan, sin, anything, or anyone else can do to steal God's affections toward us or suspend his commitment to his people. He is unwavering. Your own imperfections and sin won't stand in the way of God's affection, because of Jesus. When you put your faith in him, Jesus actively intercedes and stands in the gap *publicly* on your behalf—he stands before the Father himself as your great defender.

In the same way, you have promised to love your wife despite her imperfections. You are also called to love her as Christ loved the church. As you make your affections for her obvious to others in the interest of protecting her honor and guarding your marriage, you are her earthly defender. Let Christ's unfailing intercession before the throne remind you that your place is secure in heaven. Then, let his love and commitment fuel your own love and commitment to your bride. Let your affections for her be known; when you do, she'll feel honored, cherished, and adored.

REFLECT

Why is it beneficial to make your love for your wife obvious to those outside your marriage?

How often do you think of your wife throughout the day? Do you speak lovingly of her to those you interact with?

How can you mention your bride more intentionally and naturally in daily conversations?

PRAY

Thank God for all the things you love about your wife, and for help in making her a consistent part of daily conversations.

Pursuit 18

ACT

◷ ◷ ◷ | $ $ $

If you're into social media, post five things you love about your wife online (on Facebook, Instagram, or your social media network of choice). Do it in a way that is genuine and natural for you (no need to feel cheesy). If social media isn't your thing, write your wife a note and read it to her out loud.

___ *Check here when you've completed this pursuit.*

FIELD NOTES

Thoughts, feelings, or observations about today's pursuit?

HEADS-UP!

Tomorrow you'll need time to be spontaneous. Make sure you both create enough margin in your schedules to accommodate.

I will speak often and lovingly of my wife; this is the best adultery repellent known to man.

MICHAEL HYATT

DAY

19

Spurring Spontaneity

*And I commend joy, for man has nothing better under the sun
but to eat and drink and be joyful, for this will go with him in
his toil through the days of his life that God has
given him under the sun.*

ECCLESIASTES 8:15

For better or worse, I'm an opportunistic traveler. I like to keep regular tabs on flight rates to destinations on our "to-explore" list. It's weirdly fun and relaxing, and sometimes rewarding!

The best deal I've ever scored was a pair of round-trip tickets from Seattle to Munich for about one fourth of the regular price. Selena and I had been dreaming of going to Europe on a backpacking trip for years, but we could never pull it off financially. This opportunity changed that. Without even thinking, I booked the tickets and just like that, we were headed to Europe! Countdown to departure: twelve days.

I had planned on surprising Selena for Valentine's Day, so all I had to do was keep my mouth shut for about a week before telling her. Except, there were a few complications . . .

It occurred to me soon after booking our flights that neither of us had asked for or received time off from work. My job was pretty flexible, so my vacation request was approved without issue. I wasn't sure Selena's job at the time (she worked at an engineering firm) would be as easy. Since it was a surprise, I called her boss and practically begged him to let her take the time off. Thankfully, he did!

A few weeks later, we landed in Munich with nothing but two backpacks, a map, and plenty of nervous excitement. We had no plans, no smart phones, and no idea what to expect, but that was the beauty of it! We had no agenda but adventure, and no destination but the journey itself. We ended up visiting seven cities in five countries, made new friends, saw new sights, and created unforgettable memories. We still talk about the crazy experiences we had!

Of course, not every spontaneous adventure involves a trip across the Atlantic Ocean. We're much more likely (and just as happy) to hop in the car on a Friday evening and just start driving. Sometimes we end up at a hotel, other times we just grab dinner and head back home. The destination, mode of transportation, and details are never the same, but there is always one thing in common: *we're together.*

Every day you and your wife share is truly a gift from God. Today's challenge is all about embracing that gift. As Solomon wrote, joy is commendable and "man has nothing better under the sun but to eat and drink and be joyful." While Solomon was being fairly clear, that passage begs further explanation. Eating, drinking, and being joyful are not worthy ultimate pursuits for their own sake. Instead, Solomon was highlighting the unique positioning of the hearts of those whose trust is in God.

If you've put your trust in Jesus, unconditional and abundant joy is yours to have. This is not to say that you will never face trials or hardship, but rather that your eternal context—your secure salvation and redemption in Christ—enables you to rest easy and enjoy life's simple pleasures in profound ways that are unavailable to non-believers.

That's why we've come to enjoy spontaneity so much! When you're spontaneous, your pursuit is pure. There's no agenda but being together. When you're on an open-ended adventure with your wife, the destination is secondary. It's all about the journey. When the journey *is* the destination, you're free to simply *be* in the moment together.

As you pursue your bride, never forget your eternal context and the joy to which you're entitled as children of God. Pursue her by initiating spontaneous excursions. Whether you're venturing out locally or internationally, you'll inevitably find yourselves in the same place: growing closer together, enjoying life in God's grace, and making unforgettable memories.

REFLECT

Are you and your wife spontaneous people? Why or why not? Of the two of you, who's most likely to do something unexpected?

How can you be more spontaneous together? Consider listing a few dream adventures—big or small—to get you thinking.

PRAY

Pray for release from worry that would keep you from being spontaneous. Ask God for provision and grace in circumstances to make this happen.

Pursuit 19

ACT
○○○ | $$$

Do something spontaneous! Point at a spot on a map, grab ice cream, or just go for a walk. Do something unplanned.

If you feel a bit more adventurous, "plan" a spontaneous weekend or just get in the car and drive. No hotel reservations, no destination, just each other. Explain to your bride that she is the objective: it doesn't matter what you do or where you end up as long as you're together.

(If your wife is doing the 31-Day Pursuit Challenge on the same schedule, you can look forward to her initiating spontaneity about a week from now.)

___ *Check here when you've completed this pursuit.*

FIELD NOTES

Thoughts, feelings, or observations about today's pursuit?

DAY

20

New Frontiers

*Every good gift and every perfect gift is from above, coming
down from the Father of lights with whom there is no variation
or shadow due to change.*

JAMES 1:17

I don't know how to spell my own name. It's ridiculous, I know,
but I'm serious.

Before you judge me too harshly, let me explain. The issue is
the spelling of my middle name: which is either Glen or Glenn.
I've seen it spelled both ways on two very official documents. I'm
named after my grandpa on my mom's side, but I don't know
how to spell his name either. I've asked my mother, who says
she's 99.9 percent sure it's spelled *Glen*. But, even 0.01 percent
doubt isn't small enough to effectively assuage my uncertainty.

I've actually never really known how to spell my name, but I
only realized it a few years back. My point is that there are still
things I'm learning about myself! That's especially true when I

factor in how God has changed my heart, how having children has transformed my priorities, and how learning to love Selena continues to expose my selfishness, challenge my flesh, and refine me daily (just to name a few examples). If I could talk to myself ten years ago, it would be like talking to a completely different person. You probably feel the same way.

If that's the case for you, imagine how much you still have to learn about your wife! It's easy in marriage to assume we know all there is to know about each other. The reality is that you both change—a lot. Interests change, beliefs are refined, priorities shift, and your personalities evolve. Even couples who have been married for fifty years admit to learning new things about their spouses regularly. This is because life is in constant flux: circumstances, people, and countless other factors all contribute to how we develop and adapt as people. As Heraclitus said, "No man ever steps in the same river twice." Everything changes. Well, almost.

As followers of Christ we can agree that everything changes, barring one massive exception: God never changes. As James wrote in today's Scripture, with the Father "there is no variation or shadow due to change." What a wonderful, reassuring relief! No matter how much we change or how far life shifts, God never changes. He is the same God today that he was during creation. He will be the same God in a thousand years that he is today. Incredible!

Now ponder this for a minute: today's Scripture tells us that the unchanging, good, and gracious God of the Bible saw fit to give "every good gift and perfect gift" to us, an imperfect people prone to change. That's *pursuit*. Even in light of eternity—which he sees in full view, outside of time—God sent his Son to die so that we can be reconciled. But he doesn't stop there; as James said, every good gift comes from God. Beyond the gift of Jesus, he showers believers with even more than the bare necessities for salvation: he gives us joy, peace, hope, and love. He provides for our needs, and he graciously allows fulfillment of some of our wants. And finally for you, a husband, he has given you a wife—God's most obvious blessing in your life!

Your wife is a good gift from God, and one you will never stop unwrapping. She's multifaceted, complex, and ever changing. She is not the same woman today that she will be in a year. Even more, God is as much at work in her as he is in you! One of the best ways you can pursue your bride is by staying curious. Keep up on how she's changing by engaging in intentional conversations. Pursue her mind; ask her open-ended questions about what she thinks. Perk up your ears as she reflects and processes events in the world, your community, and in your immediate lives. Take note as you learn how her preferences have evolved. Watch diligently to perceive what God is doing in her heart. Finally, when in doubt, learn by asking questions.

No matter how familiar you feel or think you are with your wife, you will spend your entire life getting to know her. God is continually sanctifying her (and you), and that's why God has given you the gift and privilege to experience your journeys together. Enjoy them! Stay curious, and remember that every new discovery you make is a new opportunity to love her as Christ loved the church.

REFLECT

How have you seen your wife change and grow since your wedding day? List at least three ways, and be as specific as possible.

How do you think she'll change in the next five years? Ten years?

PRAY

Pray for insight and to see your wife with new eyes. Thank God for making her the way she is.

ACT ⊙⊙⊙ | $ $ $

Set aside thirty minutes this evening where you can venture to discover at least three new things about your wife. Learn something new about her story, her preferences, or how she thinks.

Start by asking open-ended questions or prompting her to recall a specific part of her childhood. If the conversation leads, try and share three things she may not know about you.

___ *Check here when you've completed this pursuit.*

FIELD NOTES

Thoughts, feelings, or observations about today's pursuit?

HEADS-UP!

On Day 24, you will be recreating your first date (or favorite date ever). You may want to start thinking about what you'll do.

DAY

21

Leading in Reading

As the rain and the snow come down from heaven
and do not return there but water the earth,
making it bring forth and sprout,
giving seed to the sower and bread to the eater,
so shall my word be that goes out from my mouth;
it shall not return to me empty,
but it shall accomplish that which I purpose,
and shall succeed in the thing for which I sent it.

ISAIAH 55:10–11

The idea of pursuit simply means chasing after another. When you pursue your wife, you earnestly chase after her heart as a means of expressing your devotion and love. Pretty intuitive, right? Ironically, one of the best ways you can pursue your wife is by leading her well.

Leadership in the household is a dense topic, and entire books are devoted to it. Indeed, every husband could spend a lifetime learning exactly what it means to love and lead his wife (and family) as Christ loves the church! For that reason, I'd like to zero in on what I believe is the clearest and most powerful way you can lead your bride: by reading God's Word together.

Nothing—truly, nothing—has transformed my own marriage more than reading Scripture with my wife. Reading the Bible together has unified us as a couple by strengthening our trust in God, deepening our affection for Jesus, growing our understanding of the gospel, and convicting us in areas of our hearts and lives where God needs to work.

It's easy to take the Bible for granted, but it's mind-blowing when you think about what it actually is! As you grasp a Bible in your hands, you are holding the very words of God himself. It's unlike every other book on the planet—its contents are not imagined in human minds or penned solely by human hands. We must accept it for what it is, "not as the word of men but as what it really is, the word of God" (1 Thessalonians 2:13).

It's vital to remember that God's Word is the primary way he has chosen to reveal himself to his people. Every time you read it, you are hearing the very voice of God and encountering the Creator of the universe! And whenever you encounter God, you leave a changed man.

Just as reading Scripture changes you individually, studying it together transforms you and your wife simultaneously. Countless times I've grown doubtful, tired, and afraid, but Selena has lovingly stepped in to remind me of a verse we've read together. Her faith informs and stretches my own; and mine does the same to hers. As you study God's Word together, you gain a common vision of reality—you can now view life through the same lens. Every trial, success, decision, and conundrum now has context—a framework—for how you can proceed in faith and obedience.

If you're doubting your ability to lead your wife in studying the Bible, don't worry. Leading your wife in this area doesn't require an advanced theological degree. Any time you pore over Scripture and let it read you (as opposed to you simply reading it), the Holy Spirit does the hard work of changing hearts. As today's Scripture reading states, God's Word never returns without accomplishing its purpose. Additionally, Hebrews 4:12 reinforces the power of God's Word:

> *"For the word of God is living and active, sharper than any two-edged sword, piercing to the division of soul and of spirit, of joints and of marrow, and discerning the thoughts and intentions of the heart."*

Pursue your bride by reading God's Word together. Lead her to the throne of God and walk alongside her to the foot of the cross. Nothing you can do for your wife is more profound or more loving than leading her toward a deeper relationship with Jesus. And the clearest and most powerful way to do just that is by reading God's Word together.

REFLECT

What are the benefits of reading God's Word *together* rather than separately?

How can you better lead your bride in studying the Bible and trusting what it says?

PRAY

Ask God for insight when reading his Word. Also pray for help in prioritizing the Word in your life and in your marriage.

Pursuit 21

ACT   ⊙⊙⊙ | $ $ $

Read at least one chapter of the Bible together. Spend time discussing what it says and how it applies to you individually and as a married couple. How does it apply to a specific situation you're facing? How can it affect your response?

If you need an idea of where to start, try the book of John, Psalm 40, Romans 8, or 1 Corinthians 13. When you're done, discuss what it might look like for you to read Scripture together on a regular basis.

___ *Check here when you've completed this pursuit.*

FIELD NOTES

Thoughts, feelings, or observations about today's pursuit?

DAY

22

No Strings Attached

[Love] does not insist on its own way.

1 CORINTHIANS 13:5

By nature, love desires closeness on every level. Touch is one way to express that desire, but sometimes wives can feel like it comes with an agenda.

When Selena and I were first married, we enjoyed full freedom of intimacy. Neither of us had experienced sex prior to our wedding night, so, needless to say, we were primed and ready to "exercise our conjugal rights." Everything was new and exciting—just as it should have been! But something changed . . .

As a young husband, I pursued my wife physically without hesitation—and as I recall, it didn't bother her a bit! But I made the mistake of pursuing her often with "the end goal" in mind. Sure, I didn't expect sex every time we kissed or hugged, but I soon realized that more involved touching—back rubs, foot massages, and long snuggles on the couch—usually only happened as a precursor to sex. Neither of us realized the pattern we were creating. Over time, even small kisses felt like they were laced with ulterior motives.

My selfishness created a pattern that made physical affection predictable and burdensome for Selena. I hadn't yet learned to pursue her first during and through intimacy instead of seeking my own desires as a top priority. Bear in mind, I'm not referring to me taking the time and effort necessary to give her an enjoyable sexual experience (that would be a different conversation entirely). I'm talking about how I caused her to feel like a *means to an end*, as opposed to showing her that she, as a person, was the ultimate end that I truly desired.

You may be familiar with Dr. Gary Chapman's book, *The 5 Love Languages.*[5] In case you're not, here's the gist: Dr. Chapman reveals the five most common languages couples "speak" to feel and express love: words of affirmation, acts of service, receiving gifts, quality time, and physical touch. Based on our interactions with couples, most husbands quickly identify physical touch as their primary love language, while wives often select one of the other four (though not always).

We've come to realize, however, that many women do desire and enjoy physical touch as an expression of love, but they've grown weary with how it's expressed in their marriage. Like Selena, those wives haven't grown tired of physical touch itself; instead they've grown weary of *selfishness*.

In Paul's famous description of love, he turned the ancient (and modern, for that matter) understanding of love on its head with one concise phrase: "[Love] does not insist on its own way." We, who have heard that phrase hundreds of times, can take the concept of selfless love for granted. But it was truly revolutionary, and indeed it still is! Selfish love isn't actually love at all—selfish love rages against everything real love stands for.

Jesus embodied the type of selfless love we are called to as husbands. He did not insist on his own way, but rather he submitted to the Father with gladness and purpose. Because of love, he took up the cross and suffered for our redemption. The experience of Christ's selfless love fuels every act of selfless love you can show to your bride.

As a husband, your call is to lead your bride by serving her. Servant leadership is always selfless leadership—even when it comes to physical touch. How can you love your wife selflessly in how you show her physical affection? More importantly, how loved will she feel if you initiate a loving touch without expecting anything in return?

REFLECT

What kinds of non-sexual touches does your wife enjoy most?
List at least three.

How can you initiate physical affection so your bride feels most
loved? Should you communicate intentionally first?

PRAY

Ask God for insight into the ways your wife feels love and for
release from previous baggage the issue of "touch" may carry in
your relationship.

Pursuit 22

ACT

⊙⊙⊙ | $ $ $

Show affection to your wife through physical touch, but approach it in a way she will enjoy it most. It could be a simple hand-hold, a foot rub, or an ad hoc back massage. Do your best to help her feel like there are "no strings attached." Remember: her enjoyment is your first and *only* priority.

___ *Check here when you've completed this pursuit.*

FIELD NOTES

Thoughts, feelings, or observations about today's pursuit?

HEADS-UP!

In two days you will be recreating either your first (or favorite) date. Now may be a good time to start planning accordingly.

DAY
23

Putting the Thought in Thoughtfulness

In this the love of God was made manifest among us, that God sent his only Son into the world, so that we might live through him. In this is love, not that we have loved God but that he loved us and sent his Son to be the propitiation for our sins. Beloved, if God so loved us, we also ought to love one another.

1 JOHN 4:9–11

I'm not a natural romantic, but a little while back I decided to try and change that.

A husband's ability to love his wife well greatly depends on his intentional, ongoing pursuit of *who* she is and understanding what she's feeling. That's the essence of romance: intentional pursuit. Romance—real romance—has less to do with what you do, and way more to do with *why* you do it.

I love my wife more than any other person on earth. You probably feel the same way about your wife (why else would you be reading this book?). I naturally show my wife love through words of encouragement and acts of service, but, tragically, my pursuit often ends there.

By God's grace, he opened my heart and helped me understand that there is more to showing Selena my love than saying "I love you" and doing chores around the house. Both of those activities are good—and included in this book—but there's still more. Genuine pursuit goes even deeper.

For a couple of years, I participated in a guys' cohort that met every other week to discuss theology, church, and stirring our hearts for Jesus. Each meeting involved answering discussion questions with brutal honesty, reminding each other of the gospel (I need daily reminding), and praying together. After about a year of meeting, we started a marriage study that entailed watching video sessions and reading *The Meaning of Marriage* by Timothy and Kathy Keller. God used that tiny community of six men to radically transform my heart and forever change how I love my bride.

It took exactly one week of our marriage study for God to bring me to my knees in repentance. As we were going through the first session, I was violently confronted with my own selfishness—my tendency to prioritize myself and my desires over my wife's. My brand of selfishness isn't always obvious, but it's there. God exposed a blind spot in my heart where I could love her better; he showed me how I could pursue her as Christ pursues me.

In one video, two wise men shared that, as husbands, we must pursue our wives with tenacity and boldness—a concept I assumed I already understood. But they opened my eyes to the deeper meaning of it—to the deeper meaning of pursuit. Two specific modes of pursuit they described were "discovering her deepest joys" and "providing the safety she desires" through my countenance, communication, and leadership.

One of the reflection questions hit me square in the face:

> Are there are new habits, attitudes, or rhythms you would like to adopt in light of this session?

Here's what I wrote as my answer:

> Conscious selflessness: going OUT OF MY WAY [sic] to think of Selena. Looking for ways to discover her joys and give her safety and comfort. Looking for ways to surprise her with adoration, generosity, and love.

The two phrases above where my heart felt particularly stirred were "conscious selflessness" and "looking for ways." In short, I finally realized (after more than a decade of marriage) what it really meant to be thoughtful. Thoughtfulness is the result of an active, selfless pursuit.

Ultimate thoughtfulness is embodied by Christ on the cross. Who went more out of their way to love than him? Who came further, served more recklessly, and sacrificed more radically than he did? Jesus had literally nothing to gain by going to the cross except the hearts of believers. Incredible!

Consider today's passage again carefully: "God sent his only Son into the world, so that we might live through him. In this is love, not that we have loved God but that he loved us and sent his Son to be the propitiation for our sins. Beloved, if God so loved us, we also ought to love one another."

If you're reading this and feeling a stirring in your soul, God is at work. He is challenging you to love more selflessly, more radically, and more thoughtfully. The thing about thoughtfulness is that there are no shortcuts or substitutes. You can't buy it and you can't fake it. Since that's the case, it is perhaps one of the most potent ways you can pursue your bride. Follow the detours thoughtfulness affords! Go out of your way to find an untraveled path to your wife's heart. As you do, you'll be pursuing your wife in the same way you are pursued by God himself.

REFLECT

What past thoughtful acts has your wife responded to best? Why do you think she responded the way she did?

How else can you be thoughtful of your bride? What do you think will speak to her most?

PRAY

Pray for inspiration to discover your wife's heart in a new way.

Pursuit 23

ACT   ⊙⊙⊙ | $ $ $

Do something thoughtful for your wife. It could be breakfast in bed, a gift, a small gesture, a short meaningful text, or an act of service. You decide.

The only requirement is that you go out of your way to do something that makes your bride feel loved and pursued.

___ *Check here when you've completed this pursuit.*

FIELD NOTES

Thoughts, feelings, or observations about today's pursuit?

HEADS-UP!

For tomorrow's pursuit, you're tasked with recreating your first or favorite date. Now is the time to finalize your plans!

DAY
24

First or Favorite

The steadfast love of the LORD never ceases;
his mercies never come to an end;
they are new every morning;
great is your faithfulness.

LAMENTATIONS 3:22–23

Our first date brought me to the brink of a biker beatdown in downtown Seattle. Neither of us will soon forget what happened that day.

We had just had our "defining the relationship" talk and officially started dating, so I invited Selena to go on a spontaneous adventure to a park in Seattle. I was sixteen years old and seven months into driving—as green as they come. Despite safely travelling thirty miles to that point, we almost died on the last turn before reaching our destination. It was a left turn, but not at an intersection; it was the kind where you had to stay in the center lane and wait for a long enough opening to cross traffic safely.

After a few minutes of waiting, my patience was rewarded. Alas! An opening revealed itself. I began the turn just like I had countless times before: release the brake, apply the gas, ease off the clutch. Up until that point I considered myself a stick-shift aficionado, but something about having a pretty girl in the car and driving in a congested city caused my brain to backfire worse than the 1994 Honda Civic that had carried us there.

As I started the turn, my left leg seemed to spasm and jerked off the clutch, killing the engine. My nightmare became reality, but not before nudging us into oncoming traffic. We were sitting ducks. My chosen traffic gap was not a generous one; there was little room for error and certainly no time to kill the engine. Selena's eyes widened as she gripped the handle above her window. She didn't scream—you know, to maintain first-date decorum and all—but I could almost hear her panicked thoughts.

I scrambled to restart the car, but I wasn't fast enough. Right about the time I realized I wouldn't get out of the way in time, oncoming traffic realized the same. A gruff bearded fellow on a Harley Davidson mashed on his brakes and fishtailed just enough to miss us. He squealed by right as I restarted the car and bolted out of harm's way . . . or so I thought.

Our new biker friend wanted to give me a piece of his mind, and perhaps a taste of his right fist. He sped around the block and intercepted us just a few hundred yards down the road. Shocked, and a little afraid, I pulled over to see what he wanted. I quickly realized that we had an irreconcilable conflict of interest. He wanted to bash my face in, and I wanted very much to keep my face as un-bashed-in as possible. So I did the brave boy-friend thing and locked all the doors. After a barrage of threats, cuss words, and angry gestures, he finally left. I thanked God for a strong driver's side door.

The rest of our first date was even more unforgettable than the beginning! Minutes after arriving at the park, we found ourselves enthralled in an impromptu, all-out blackberry fight. I can't recall exactly how it started, but we both ended up fully submerged in the lake (in our normal clothes) and covered from head to toe in blackberry stains.

What made that day so unforgettable? Peculiarly enough, it's not the biker incident we remember first; it's the blackberries. But even more than the blackberries, we remember laughing and having fun with each other. We remember what it felt like to be together for the first time, with fresh eyes and hearts full of new affection and knowledge of each other. Sharing in the experience—the activities, the feelings, the newness—is what made our first date memorable. Being together is what makes life memorable.

Married life has a way of growing routine. In many ways, it can be the antithesis of the first date: the daily grind, mundane moments, and repetitive realities. Routines aren't bad! Real life happens in the small moments. Sustainable joy comes from finding contentment and purpose in Christ during life's in-between times.

Following Jesus is a lot like a marriage. The first time you heard the gospel and placed your trust in him, it was an exhilarating and new relationship. Every believer who stays the course will experience "valleys," where zeal feels nonexistent and devotion alone fuels progress. During those times, we must find unshakable joy in the unchanging promises of God throughout Scripture. Words like those in today's verse, "his mercies never come to an end; they are new every morning," exist to fill us with fresh hope and stir our affection. Reading those words is almost like recalling a first-date experience. Christ's love and mercies never grow old; they're new every morning. He never grows tired of loving you. Each promise in Scripture is almost like a walk down memory lane. It's like God is saying, "Don't forget what I promised, and always remember my affection as if it's the first day we met."

Do you remember your first date? Even if you didn't do something crazy or formal, you had "new eyes" for each other. Today's challenge is all about recalling your very first date as vividly as possible. Every relationship has an exciting beginning and less-than-exciting moments somewhere in the middle. Celebrate your history! Sometimes your past can fuel your present pursuit.

REFLECT

Recall your first ever or favorite past date. What made it so enjoyable for you? What made it enjoyable for your wife?

What about that date can be revisited in the future? Write down a few ideas for fun dates and tuck them away for future reference.

PRAY

Thank God for your unique history. Pray that he gives you new eyes for each other and a fresh sense of pursuit in your marriage.

Pursuit 24

ACT   ☺☺☺ | ???

Today's challenge is a big one, but you can do it! Do your
best to re-create your first (or favorite) date ever, step-by-
step. If that's not feasible, plan a time and a place where
you can meet as if it's your first date, then go from there.
Depending on how elaborate you make it, you may want
to use today to begin planning your date for the near
future. Don't delay. Have fun, be creative, and celebrate
your history!

*(If your wife is doing her own 31-Day Pursuit Challenge, she'll be
reading about the same topic today. Consider planning together!)*

___ *Check here when you've completed this pursuit.*

FIELD NOTES

Thoughts, feelings, or observations about today's pursuit?

DAY

25

Playful Pursuit

God has not destined us for wrath, but to obtain salvation
through our Lord Jesus Christ, who died for us so that whether
we are awake or asleep we might live with him. Therefore
encourage one another and build one another up,
just as you are doing.

1 Thessalonians 5:9–11

Having children has taught me the importance of play. Experts claim that children often learn the most through play. Although we're no longer children physically, we are children of God, and I would reckon that we still learn a lot through play. Play is powerful, and, as adults, it's easy to forget what it feels like to get lost in fun—to follow whimsy and curiosity to their very end with carefree innocence. Can you recall the last time you got completely lost in an activity? (Your phone doesn't count.) Have you ever resigned your full attention so wholeheartedly to something fun that you forgot it would end? Those moments are rare, and the challenge against them is more intense today than ever before.

Modern distractions abound, and everything seems to compete for our attention: screens, pings, notifications, vibrations, messages, e-mails, headlines, tweets, sound bytes, podcasts, on-demand entertainment, music, billboards, apps, flash sales… the list goes on and on. It's exhausting!

Your attention is the new currency, and it's incredibly valuable. Marketers have figured out that if they can grab your attention, they have a chance at your affection. If they can win your affection, they might be able to convince your mind. Finally, if they can convince your mind, they have a pretty good shot at your wallet.

I, for one, am flattered that they think my attention is worth so much! But in all sincerity, if our attention is so valuable, we must spend it wisely. Every attention-grabbing intrusion into your life wars against how you were created to exist: present, focused, undistracted, and with intentionality.

Given its value, what would happen if we "saved up" our attention and spent it only on what matters most? Transformation would happen. As followers of Christ, our best use of attention is in worship and service of God. As husbands, our next best use of attention is in loving, serving, and getting to know our wives.

In today's passage, the apostle Paul closes his first letter to the Thessalonians by urging them to stay alert—to be attentive to God and the gospel they received: "Let us not sleep, as others do, but let us keep awake" (1 Thessalonians 5:6). He's reminding them to spend their time and focus—*their attention*—on what matters most: worshipping and obeying God, because Jesus will return unexpectedly. Then something interesting happens. Paul then turns their gaze toward each other. He says, "Encourage one another and build one another up, just as you are doing" (v. 11). Paul is urging them toward genuine community and authentic brotherhood. He's telling them to be friends.

This is where play comes in. Play is perhaps one of the fastest and most meaningful ways to build friendship. Encouraging words have a place, but the heart is most encouraged by engaged friendship. Playing is a gift and a skill useful for strengthening and deepening the bonds of friendship.

If play is an irreplaceable tool for building friendship, and as humans we are created for relationship with God and each other, then it follows that play is irreplaceable. Playing is necessary for relational health. As a husband you can lead your family in this and have a blast doing it; but it only happens when you spend your attention intentionally.

Ralph Waldo Emerson said, "It is a happy talent to know how to play."[6] Spend your attention learning how to play with your wife; build your friendship. Be intentional about enjoying each other's company, shutting out distraction, and having fun together. You and your wife will never regret spending focused, undistracted time playing together.

REFLECT

Think of a time in the past when you've been lost in play. What made that activity so fun?

How can you and your wife play together regularly? List at least three ideas.

PRAY

Ask God for inspiration and ways to see play happening around you that you can duplicate in your life. Pray for help in creating a playful, loving marriage culture that glorifies him.

Pursuit 25

ACT

◐ ◓ ◑ | $ $ $

Play a game together. Chess, checkers, cribbage, Uno, Twister, whatever your favorite game is, set aside at least thirty minutes to play it with your wife. Clear your schedule if needed!

___ *Check here when you've completed this pursuit.*

FIELD NOTES

Thoughts, feelings, or observations about today's pursuit?

HEADS-UP!

This is a big heads-up. You're nearing the end of this 31-Day Pursuit Challenge, and the last day is designed to be your grandest gesture yet. Go ahead and take a look at the final pursuit to get an idea of what's in store. Then get to work!

It is a happy talent
to know how to play.

RALPH WALDO EMERSON

DAY
26

Encouragement Grounded in the Gospel

Let each of us please his neighbor for his good, to build him up.
For Christ did not please himself, but as it is written,
"The reproaches of those who reproached you fell on me."
For whatever was written in former days was written for our
instruction, that through endurance and through the encourage-
ment of the Scriptures we might have hope.

ROMANS 15:2–4

A little over two weeks ago (on Day 10), we explored the idea of extravagant encouragement. Today, I'd like to take our conversation a little further. No one can encourage me like Selena. She has an uncanny ability to diffuse stress and infuse me with energy—her words, her actions, her belief in me, and her touch all act like adrenaline shots in the arm. She can also have the opposite effect; it's definitely a double-edged sword.

Everyone will agree that encouragement should be practiced

regularly in a healthy marriage. The key word there is *practiced*. Have you ever wondered why your wife doesn't always respond as you'd expect when you tell her she looks beautiful or that you're proud of her? Encouraging words don't always accomplish their desired purpose. They don't always work. Good and helpful encouragement requires skill, and skill only comes with repetition, good form, and frequency—or, *practice*.

Effective encouragement fills its recipient with courage. Ineffective encouragement misses that mark. If you're at all like me, you can easily recall many times when you've encouraged your wife ineffectively. As husbands, it's part of our job to figure out what encouragement speaks loudest to our wives and make that a regular part of our marriages.

The absolute best way to encourage your wife is by reminding her of the gospel and helping her refocus her eyes on Jesus. It's coming alongside her, empathizing with her circumstance, and speaking intentional words that are grounded in the good news of Jesus. He alone provides the boundless hope, peace, and joy we so desperately need. When you point your wife toward Christ, you point her down the path of life.

How can I tangibly point my wife toward Jesus? The most tangible encouragement for God's people is in his Word. Today's Scripture says, "Whatever was written in former days was written for our instruction, that through endurance and through the encouragement of the Scriptures we might have hope." Whenever you remind your wife of God's promises in the Bible, you're letting his very words fill her with hope and courage.

Pursue your bride's heart and mind by asking questions and listening carefully to her answers. If she's struggling with something, find out what and why. Be tactful so she doesn't feel interrogated, but do your best to learn as many details as possible. Then, fill her with courage and faith by pointing her to God's promises in the Bible. That's where the skill comes in.

The best way to build your skill level in this area—and your skill as an encouraging husband—is to know and understand the Bible well. Learn to love God's Word! All Scripture is God breathed (2 Timothy 3:16), it's alive and active (Hebrews 4:12), and it builds believers up in faith and hope (Acts 20:32, Romans 10:17). How can you pray and speak applicable, helpful Scriptures and promises over her if you don't know where they are or what they mean?

Pursue your bride by pursuing a deeper understanding of God's Word. Let it bear weight and authority in your life in increasing measure. Pray that it transforms you and fills you with wisdom and discernment. Then, as a husband, you will be equipped with the best source of encouragement in the universe: the very words of God himself!

REFLECT

What promises from the Bible has someone spoken over you in the past that you found encouraging?

How might your wife be encouraged by a particular Scripture? What issues and concerns are regularly on her mind that you can speak life-giving Scripture over?

PRAY

Pray for wisdom and discernment when reading God's Word. Ask for discipline in setting aside committed time to spend in the Word by yourself.

ACT

⊙⊙⊙ | $ $ $

Find a verse with the sole purpose of encouraging your wife. Write it down in a note and give it to her at the start of the next day. Consider including a written prayer for her in the note.

After she's read the note, explain to her why God's Word is the best encouragement you can speak over each other. Discuss ways to make it more central in your lives.

____ *Check here when you've completed this pursuit.*

FIELD NOTES

Thoughts, feelings, or observations about today's pursuit?

DAY
27

Good Ground Rules

Let no corrupting talk come out of your mouths, but only such
as is good for building up, as fits the occasion, that it may give
grace to those who hear.

Ephesians 4:29

It seems like marriage is just another word for "endlessly learning to communicate." Yes, there is so much more to marriage than communication, but how many marital issues would be erased or solved if we just learned to communicate in a healthier manner? As a husband, you can pursue your bride by leading the charge in establishing healthy communication ground rules.

The most critical component of healthy communication is perseverance. Both you and your wife should never quit; talk through every conflict until you reach the other side. The biggest temptation when facing tough communication is to run—to bail out and avoid the issue. This may feel better in the moment, but if you do that often enough, the waste builds up and poisons your entire marriage.

Thus, a good first ground rule for healthy communication is this: resolve to persevere and talk through everything. Of course, perseverance requires grit and determination, but if you both have a unified understanding of what healthy communication looks like, pushing through the process is much (much) easier. Otherwise, unhealthy communication habits will only leave you feeling exhausted, beat up, and defeated.

It's impossible to address everything everyone should or shouldn't say in every possible situation. The Bible doesn't even do as much—at least not explicitly. God calls us to use wisdom, to speak in love, as today's verse instructs, and to let "no corrupting talk come out of [our] mouths." God's Word may not deal with every possible argument you will face in marriage, but it deals with the heart. Jesus knows that if he has our hearts, he has our tongues. Additionally, Jesus gives us the power and counsel of the Holy Spirit to help us act with wisdom, even in the middle of a heated argument.

In light of how God has equipped us—with His Word and the Holy Spirit—it's most helpful to speak generally about marital communication and apply discernment and wisdom from there. When creating communication ground rules, I recommend using three categories for what you say and how you say it: off-limits, unhelpful and unproductive, and wise. Let's explore.

Off-limits. Some words and phrases will never help your marriage, so they fall into the off-limits category. This includes name-calling, insults, demeaning or abusive language and tones, and expressing ideas aimed solely at destroying your marriage. If you can't say it in love, it shouldn't be said. Examples of toxic ideas are using the threat of divorce, phrases like "I should have married so-and-so," and "I knew marrying you was a mistake." Specifically defining off-limits vocabulary creates agreement about what's fair before an argument erupts.

Unhelpful and unproductive. This kind of communication isn't necessarily malicious, but it doesn't produce fruit or kindle love between you and your wife. A big one for us is the flippant use of absolutes. "You always" and "You never" statements are rarely accurate or helpful. They're lazy. Other dismissive language also falls into this category. Saying "Whatever" under your breath before leaving the room is an apt example of passive, dismissive, unhelpful language. It does nothing to move you toward recon- ciliation, which is God's mandate for healthy conflict resolution.

Wise. Finally, wisdom compels us to act in ways that are life giving and marriage preserving. Many arguments between Selena and me could have been avoided or handled productively if only we'd had them at a wise time and in the appropriate place. For example, late at night when you're both exhausted is prob- ably not the best time to get into the nuances of how sexually frustrated you are in your marriage. Letting loose at the in-laws' house isn't the best place to finally express to your wife how and why they drive you crazy. Create boundaries around when and where you'll engage in tough conversations, and learn to be okay with tabling them until a more ideal opportunity presents itself.

Pursue your wife by protecting your marriage from unhealthy communication. Establish healthy boundaries around what, how, and when you speak to one another. Words are powerful, and no one's words are more powerful in your marriage than those you say to each other.

REFLECT

What are some examples of "corrupting talk" you've experienced in your marriage?

Do you find it hard to control what you say when you're frustrated, tired, or angry? How can you create boundaries to protect yourself and your wife during those times?

PRAY

Ask God for discernment in the ways you already speak to each other, and for good judgment in the words you use from now on.

Pursuit 27

ACT   ☉☉☉ | $ $ $

Grab some paper and write out a set of proposed ground rules for communication in your household. Start with the three categories we covered today and fill in each one in appropriately. Be as thorough as possible.

When you're finished, sit down, discuss what you wrote, and reach a mutual understanding. Then, sign the paper together and pray for agreement as you live it out.

(If your wife is going through her own challenge, she'll be reading the same thing. Definitely craft your ground rules together.)

___ *Check here when you've completed this pursuit.*

FIELD NOTES

Thoughts, feelings, or observations about today's pursuit?

HEADS-UP!

Day 31 is just a few days away. How's planning going?

28

She Is You

*The rib that the LORD God had taken from the man he made
into a woman and brought her to the man. Then the man said,
"This at last is bone of my bones and flesh of my flesh; she shall
be called Woman, because she was taken out of Man."
Therefore a man shall leave his father and his mother and hold
fast to his wife, and they shall become one flesh.*

GENESIS 2:22–24

It's easy to gloss over today's passage, especially if you've read it
many times before. The concept of two becoming "one flesh"
is profound. We must not be too quick to dismiss its meaning,
or to assume we've understood every aspect of it. Consider two
scenarios.

During our first year of marriage, I bought a 1977 Volkswagen
bus. It was school bus yellow, and possibly the most perfect piece
of automotive art the world had ever seen. I loved this van. Sure,
she had her quirks, but those are what made her so special. For

example, the gas gauge didn't work very well, so the only way I knew I was running low on fuel was if I stopped smelling gasoline fumes. No smell, no gas. Easy enough, right?

Unfortunately, there came a time when we had to store her in a garage for a few months straight. It wasn't too long, but apparently it was enough time for the engine to stop working. At the time, we had no money, tools, or knowledge to fix her, so I said my good-byes and we parted ways. I suppose we could have scraped together the cash, but it would have cost us everything we had to get her fixed. I have few regrets in life, and selling my yellow VW bus is definitely one. It was a hard choice, but the right one.

Fast-forward ten years. We're at home and our oldest daughter—two years old at the time—was jumping on the couch. In a burst of excitement, she leaned too far and nose-dived over the back of the couch. I watched the horror unfold in slow motion; I was helplessly far away. Her forehead smashed into the hardwood floor first. The momentum of her legs carried them forward, but the floor kept her head and torso from rotating along with them. Her legs scorpioned over her back and head as far as physically possible, creating an almost inhuman form. She screamed instantly and I sprang into action.

Based on what I saw, I feared she had suffered a severe brain or neck injury. In a panic, we rushed her to the emergency room. I told the doctors to take every test and do everything necessary. There was no cost too great, no price I wouldn't pay to help her. Thank God he makes kids mostly out of fat and cartilage. A few hours later our daughter was bouncing down the sidewalk with a smile and a lollipop.

What's the difference between those two stories? The van was disposable; our daughter is not. I couldn't find two hundred dollars to fix an engine, so we got rid of it, but I'd sell everything I owned to help my own flesh and blood. She is mine, and I'd do anything—*anything*—to care for her and protect her.

Yes, a child is a vivid reminder of part of what becoming "one flesh" sexually can mean, but an equally profound miracle happens when a husband and a wife are made one flesh spiritually. Even the apostle Paul, who was intelligent and well versed in the things of God, said of two becoming one, "This mystery is profound, and I am saying that it refers to Christ and the church" (Ephesians 5:31–32). Jesus paid every cost to rescue his flesh—the church. As husbands, we are called to the same radical love and sacrifice for our brides.

Fierce husband, your wife is "flesh of your flesh" and "bone of your bone." When you stood at the altar and said "I do," you became one flesh. She is you. You are her. Now, I don't mean that literally, but as far as you're concerned, she is an extension of you, and you of her. As Paul said, "In the same way, husbands should love their wives as their own bodies. He who loves his wife loves himself" (Ephesians 5:28). Her pain is your pain and her joy is your joy. She is part of you now, and as such, there should be no limit to what you would do to preserve, protect, and care for her.

REFLECT

In your own words, describe what it means to be "one flesh" with your wife.

How can you better treat your wife as yourself? Give examples of how you can partake in her joy and help carry her burdens.

PRAY

Ask God to renew your oneness and to make you one flesh.

ACT

⏱ ◔ ◔ | $ $ $

Consider ways you can better preserve, protect, and care for your bride. Have you acted selfishly and unknowingly treated her in ways you wouldn't treat yourself? Write down five tangible ways you can love your wife "as your own body" or "as you would love yourself."

When you're finished, read and explain your list to your wife, then pray together.

____ *Check here when you've completed this pursuit.*

FIELD NOTES

Thoughts, feelings, or observations about today's pursuit?

DAY

29

Fifteen Seconds a Day

Let him kiss me with the kisses of his mouth!
For your love is better than wine.

SONG OF SOLOMON 1:2

I once met a gentleman at church named Tim. Tim and his wife had been married more than thirty years and weathered many trials (cancer included). In awe, I asked him what the secret was: "How have you stuck together for so long?" I asked him this knowing that we shared our faith and reliance on Jesus Christ.

His reply was uncomplicated: "The fifteen-second kiss."

Intrigued, I asked, "What do you mean exactly?"

"Every day, my wife and I give each other a fifteen-second kiss," Tim responded. "It's long enough that you can't fake it—it forces us to connect."

I had never heard of purposefully timing a kiss. It was a new idea, and I was anxious to give it a try! Selena and I kiss often enough, but Tim helped us realize that we don't usually kiss for more than a few seconds. I'm not exactly sure why, but I do know it wasn't like that when we were dating. I decided to propose the idea to Selena, and she agreed! (It was an easy sell.)

After three days of fifteen-second kisses, we discovered a few things. First, fifteen-seconds isn't that long . . . except when you're kissing. I know I burn through fifteen seconds all the time without thinking about it. But when you're kissing and consciously timing it, it seems much longer. And that's a good thing!

At first we were both aware of the time because of the novelty of the exercise. It didn't take long for us to get lost in the kiss. If other couples are like us, we let life get too busy to allow "getting lost" doing anything. The fifteen-second kiss was a refreshing reminder that we can truly get lost in our affection for one another.

The second thing we learned is that it's nearly impossible to kiss for an extended period of time and not feel closer to one another. Kissing is intimate. We found that as we got lost in kissing, we were getting lost together. The thing about getting lost together is that it actually helps you find one another. We were reminded how much the act of kissing makes us feel closer. Since we always want to feel closer, we purposed to make intentional kissing a daily part of our lives.

We also discovered how kissing refocuses us on who we are to each other. When you're "kissably close" to your wife, smelling her breath and feeling her skin, it helps you remember who she is as a person. In marriage, it's easy to start seeing your wife as a roommate or casual partner, but kissing her will remind you of her distinctly human qualities (good and bad) that you fell in love with in the first place.

Finally, kissing is a gateway drug. Have you ever gotten home from work without an appetite, only to have cooking aromas awaken your hunger? Kissing has a similar effect. If neither of you were "intimacy minded" before your fifteen-second kiss, there's a good chance both of you will be soon after.

As we read in today's Scripture passage, the entire book of Song of Solomon opens with a bride confessing her love. She begins by saying, "Let him kiss me with the kisses of his mouth!" Kissing is a part of their mutual pursuit from the very beginning. Kissing is intimate, kissing is powerful, and kissing is good. There is truly nothing on earth like it.

Never underestimate the power of a simple, intentional kiss to display your affection and deepen feelings of closeness in your marriage.

REFLECT

Think back on your best kiss with your spouse ever (or at least think of a memorable one). What made it so special?

How can kissing regularly and intentionally build your marriage?

PRAY

Ask God to help increase your sense of connection through daily expressions of affection.

ACT

⏱ ◔ ◑ | $ $ $

(Any idea where this is going?) It's time for a fifteen-second kiss. Go the extra mile and freshen up. Then, the next time you see your wife, tell her about the fifteen-second kiss idea and suggest you give it a try. Feel free to go longer than fifteen seconds, but certainly don't go shorter. Do your best to kiss without motive or agenda, but don't be surprised if it leads elsewhere.

(If your wife is taking her own 31-Day Pursuit Challenge, she'll be reading about kissing too. Try a thirty-second kiss . . . for science.)

____ *Check here when you've completed this pursuit.*

FIELD NOTES

Thoughts, feelings, or observations about today's pursuit?

HEADS-UP!

Two more days until the biggest pursuit so far. Gear up.

Men, you'll never be a good groom to your wife unless you're first a good bride to Jesus.

TIMOTHY KELLER

DAY
30

Self-Awareness Is Wife-Awareness

Do not be conformed to this world, but be transformed by the renewal of your mind, that by testing you may discern what is the will of God, what is good and acceptable and perfect. For by the grace given to me I say to everyone among you not to think of himself more highly than he ought to think, but to think with sober judgment, each according to the measure of faith that God has assigned.

ROMANS 12:2–3

In marriage, you will disagree often and you will argue. Both are inevitable. When you put two sinners in the same house for life, there will be conflict. We have yet to meet a married couple who has never had a fight! The question is not, "What if we fight?" but "When we fight, how can we do it in a healthy way?"

It's useless to define healthy fighting on our own. We must turn to a moral authority outside of ourselves: the Bible. Here's what it has to say about resolving conflict:

- Reconciliation is always the goal. (Matthew 5:24)
- Confession and apologizing are necessary. (Luke 17:4)
- Anger is normal, but not reason for sin. (Ephesians 4:26)
- Listen first, speak maybe, always be patient. (James 1:19)
- Forgiveness is a must. (Colossians 3:13)

How could the above principles (think of them as marching orders) transform how you handle disagreements with your wife? How could they change your heart as a husband and completely shift your motivations during an argument? To answer those questions, it's helpful to identify three typical argument sources.

The first argument source is probably the most minor: *annoyances and bickering*. If you have differing opinions about how to drive, how to do certain chores, or how to chew your food, you will probably bicker occasionally. These arguments are usually short-lived and fairly harmless—as long as they don't go on unaddressed for years and sprout into bitterness or resentment.

The second argument source is *deep emotional hurt* or bitterness. These are tougher because the heart is involved. To be transparent, I feel hurt when Selena doesn't express desire for me sexually. She has a thousand things on her mind, and sex isn't always as high on her priority list as it is on mine. I know this, but if I stew in my sexual frustration, it turns to anger. If I don't find a way to express myself lovingly, it builds up until I make a jabby comment and a fight breaks out.

The final, deepest source of arguments in marriage is *core issue disagreements.* Not every couple shares their belief in Jesus, and it causes fundamental problems. If you're always fighting with your wife over your core beliefs, pray. Only Jesus can change your heart or hers.

All disagreements result from sin, stubbornness, and selfishness in at least one of you. If there were no sin in the world or in your marriage, there would be complete harmony. Obviously that's not the case! As a husband, the best way you can pursue your bride during arguments is by practicing self-awareness.

A self-aware man understands he is imperfect in ways he may not yet perceive. He knows he needs help from the Holy Spirit and his wife to be transformed, as today's verse says, "by the renewing of his mind." He follows Paul's direction to not think of himself more highly than he ought, but rather "with sober judgment." Most importantly, a self-aware man sees himself accurately—as a sinner saved by grace—while having full view of the holy and powerful God of the universe. Finally, a self-aware man understands his desperate need for the gospel and his constant tendency to forget it.

Arguments present unique opportunities for self-awareness. In them, pursue your bride by asking yourself honest questions like, *Where can I change? Am I sinning? Have I done anything to contribute to how she's feeling?* Asking yourself questions like those defuses the me-centered thinking that intensifies the disagreement. Pursue your wife through each fight. Think of her, "look to her interests" (Philippians 2:4), and serve her through gospel-centered self-awareness.

REFLECT

Do you consider yourself a self-aware person? Why or why not?

Think back to your last argument, and answer each question:
  1. How could I have handled it differently?

  2. Was I sinning (pride, selfishness, etc.)? How?

  3. Did I do anything to contribute to her frustration or anger?

PRAY

Ask God for presence of mind during conflict, and for the Holy Spirit to work on your heart as well as your wife's.

ACT

⊙⊙⊙ | $ $ $

Part of learning about yourself means asking for help. When your home is peaceful (i.e. you're not in an argument), ask your wife to share three behaviors or tendencies of yours she'd like you to change. Make sure you're in a mental place to hear her answers without getting defensive. Reassure her that she won't start a fight, no matter what she says. Then ask God for help by praying together.

___ *Check here when you've completed this pursuit.*

FIELD NOTES

Thoughts, feelings, or observations about today's pursuit?

HEADS-UP!

Tomorrow is the big day. Ready?

DAY
31

Celebrating a
Life of Pursuit

I do not account my life of any value nor as precious to myself,
if only I may finish my course and the ministry that I received
from the Lord Jesus, to testify to the gospel of the grace of God.

ACTS 20:24

Congratulations; you've made it! While this is the end of our
journey together, today marks the beginning of the rest of your
life pursuing your wife. In the introduction, I called this book a
crutch. Odd start, I know, but I hope it all makes sense now. If
you recall, we read this quote from C. S. Lewis:

Duty is only a substitute for love (of God and of other
people) like a crutch which is a substitute for a leg. Most
of us need the crutch at times; but of course it is idiotic to
use the crutch when our own legs (our own loves, tastes,
habits etc.) can do the journey on their own. They are

helpful and necessary for a time, but eventually you need to walk without them.[7]

That's what today is all about: dropping the crutches, walking without them, and forging onward as a man in pursuit. Loving your bride out of duty is fine and sometimes necessary, but it's not the ideal. Maybe you started this book out of duty, or maybe duty is where you are today. Keep going if either is the case. But know that duty is only a substitute for love—it's a crutch to help you along when your habits and desires won't carry you. The more enjoyable route—the way you were made to operate—is to pursue your bride out of love for her that is fueled by how deeply and eternally you are loved in Christ. Hopefully every day of this challenge has brought you closer to that end.

I approached this book with two major goals in mind. First, I sought to show you the depth of Christ's love and pursuit of you, and then to illustrate how experiencing Christ's love fuels how you pursue your wife.

Second, I aimed to help you think differently about what it means to actually pursue your bride. I hope this book has helped you to grow in skill, creativity, and conviction in the ways and consistency with which you chase after the woman God gave you. That's why we're ending with today's passage—consider it my Hail Mary if I haven't succeeded to this point!

Today's verse is very dear to my heart—it's become an essential part of my daily life. It's so vital that I've written it on the wall in my office just above my computer screen. I read it aloud every morning before I start working, and any time I feel my heart straying from finding my identity, worth, and purpose in Christ. It shows me that this life isn't about me—it's about Jesus. It's a reminder that my days are fleeting and my treasure is in heaven, and that this life isn't valuable in itself. It's my daily encouragement to "finish my course and the ministry that I received from the Lord Jesus, to testify to the gospel of the grace of God."

Notice how personal Paul's language sounds. He says, "my course" and "the ministry that I received." We're not all called to emulate Paul's ministry. (For one, Paul was single and this book is for married men!) The church is made up of many members who serve different, complementary functions (1 Corinthians 12). Just as Paul had a course and a ministry, you and I have a course and a ministry. No matter your vocational calling, as husbands who follow Jesus we all share a common charge: to love, serve, and pursue our wives as Christ loved, served, and pursued the church (Ephesians 5:25).

As I mentioned, today marks a new beginning for you in fulfilling a portion of God's call on your life. If this book has accomplished its purpose, you can forge on with a fresh understanding of how to pursue your bride in light of Jesus' pursuit of you. Now's the time for you to put your new knowledge to work. It's time to drop the crutches and *walk in love* with boldness, decisiveness, and conviction.

At this point, the two biggest challenges to your pursuit are time and creativity. Will you be actively pursuing your bride one year from now? How about ten? Twenty? Will your pursuit actively change and evolve as your wife changes? By God's grace, you—*we*—will be able to answer yes to each of those questions, but it will require intentionality. That's your final challenge: to pursue your bride earnestly, lovingly, and intentionally for the rest of your life.

If you feel intimidated, don't. Rest assured that Jesus will help you every step of the way; fix your eyes on him, remember how relentlessly God pursued you in Christ, and let his love fuel your pursuit of your wife every moment until the day you die.

REFLECT

Think back over the past month. Which pursuit challenge has had the most impact on you? On your wife?

Why do you think the above challenges were particularly memorable? What do your observations say about how you can pursue your wife in the future?

PRAY

Ask God to remind you daily of his relentless pursuit—of you and your wife. Pray that he gives you renewed vision, purpose, creativity, and desire to pursue your wife in fresh, genuine ways.

Feel free to write this prayer out below (or elsewhere) and refer to it regularly as a constant reminder of this experience.

Pursuit 31

ACT   ☉ ☉ ☉ | $ $ $

Commemorate the start of your lifelong pursuit. It's time to celebrate! Do something ridiculous, extravagant, off-script, and off-the-charts unconventional. Now is your opportunity to pull out all the stops! *Hint: There are some unique date ideas in the back of this book.*

Hopefully you've taken some time to think about and plan for today (heeding the "Heads-Up!" notifications along the way). If not, don't worry—feel free to do some research and find something your wife will love.

(If your wife is going through her 31-Day Pursuit Challenge, she'll be here too. Plan together in the name of mutual pursuit.)

___ *Check here when you've completed this pursuit. Great work.*

FINAL PURSUIT CHALLENGE

Pursue your wife for the rest of your life by starting with a custom Pursuit Plan. See the following pages for details and help with this challenge.

A Lifelong Pursuit Challenge

Over the past thirty-one days, we've explored how to love our brides with selflessness, service, affection, friendship, and thoughtfulness—all in light of how Christ pursues us. I hope and pray that you and your wife have experienced change in your hearts and in your marriage.

Now you have a choice to make. You can put this book on a shelf and slowly forget all you've learned, but reminisce of the good activities you did. Or, you can let this book represent a small beginning to a much larger life of an even more radical pursuit. I'm hoping you do the latter.

Don't worry, you don't have to do it alone quite yet. I've created a basic template to help you get started. It aims to answer a few basic questions: How can you make pursuit a daily part of your life? What does your lifelong pursuit of your wife look like from this day forward? What habits will you adopt daily, weekly, monthly, and yearly?

Complete the Pursuit Plan template on the next page. Feel free to share it with your wife or get her feedback. Set reminders on your calendar and most importantly, follow through. Revisit your plan regularly to keep it up to date and fresh in your mind. Consider journaling regularly about your pursuit as a way of tracking personal and marital growth.

My Pursuit Plan

NAME _____   DATE _____

WIFE'S NAME _____

Over the course of this 31-Day Pursuit Challenge, I've learned to pursue my wife as Christ pursues me by:

Given what I've learned, I will pursue my wife consistently through the following intentional actions of love:

DAILY	WEEKLY	MONTHLY	YEARLY

Today marks the beginning of the rest of my life pursuing my wife. I understand that I am called to love her as Christ loved the church, and that doing so is my privilege as her husband. I cannot do it alone, but it won't happen without my effort. By God's grace, I will love my wife well until the day I die, and not a moment less.

SIGNED _____

50 Creative Date Ideas

I admit it. I'm not as creative as you when it comes to crafting an incredible date. After all, you know your area, your passions, and your wife better than anyone. However, here are some ideas in case you feel stuck. This list is far from ultimate, but it's a start!*

01. Complete one bucket list item for each of you.
02. Go stargazing and find at least three new constellations.
03. Get up early, grab coffee, and watch the sunrise.
04. Make a meal with *only* what you find at a farmer's market.
05. Pick a spot on a map and just start driving.
06. Try rock climbing. Do at least one dyno each.
07. Rent kayaks and go paddling.
08. Go to a jazz club and dance to *all* the slow songs.
09. Visit a zoo or an aquarium.
10. Get theatre tickets to a local play.
11. Begin training for a 5k together.
12. Get pedicures (i.e. take one for the team).
13. Go fishing and cook your catch over a fire.
14. Sign up for a cooking class.
15. See a comedy show.
16. Visit a local art gallery.
17. Go paintballing. Mutiny against everyone else.
18. Go to a trampoline park (if you can find one nearby).
19. Catch a movie at a drive-in. Kiss more than usual.
20. Go on a dessert tasting tour to three places in one night.
21. Take swing dancing lessons.

22. Go paddle boarding. Make a point to fall in the water.
23. Do something that gets your adrenaline pumping.
24. Take a rowboat out on a pond at sunset.
25. Go for a jog in the rain.
26. Volunteer at a local homeless shelter.
27. Try an improv class.
28. Plan a surprise weekend getaway.
29. Go to a new restaurant you'd normally never visit.
30. Sign up for a mud run.
31. Have a picnic in the park.
32. Head to an arcade for an old-school game tournament.
33. Check out a new band.
34. Go away for the weekend. No plans, just go.
35. Attend a local poetry reading.
36. Try a workout class neither of you has ever tried.
37. Have a bonfire on the beach. Make s'mores.
38. Visit a botanical garden.
39. Take salsa dancing lessons.
40. Go on a local used bookstore tour.
41. Do something touristy in your hometown.
42. Go to a matinee. Critique the film over lunch.
43. Take SCUBA lessons.
44. Hike a nearby trail (one you both find challenging).
45. Order takeout and play a game you both love.
46. Go ice skating. Grab cocoa nearby and people watch.
47. Visit a local landmark and have dinner nearby.
48. Ride bikes through your city and grab street tacos.
49. Get a couple's massage. Rather, give each other massages!
50. Have a night in, no phones, no distractions. Get frisky.

*All the activities on this list should be done safely and responsibly. Anything you do is at your own risk. We're not responsible for your safety! Have fun, be careful, live to tell the story.

Additional Resources

Our mission is simple: to build marriages for the glory of Christ. It drives everything we do. We release content weekly via our blog, podcast, and social media.

FIND US ONLINE

FierceMarriage.com
FierceMarriage.com/Podcast
Facebook.com/FierceMarriage
Instagram.com/FierceMarriage
YouTube.com/FierceMarriage
Twitter.com/FierceMarriage

RECOMMENDED BOOKS

For a list of books we love, visit FierceMarriage.com/Resources.

SHARE THIS BOOK WITH A FRIEND

If you'd like to share this book with a friend, please direct them to 31DayPursuit.com.

DO YOU HAVE FEEDBACK OR A STORY?

If this book has helped you, please share your story with us. If we can improve or fix anything about this resource, please let us know. To do either, send an e-mail to care@fiercemarriage.com.

WANT TO LEAVE A REVIEW?

If you've enjoyed this book, we'd be honored if you wrote an honest review whereever you purchased your copy (Amazon.com or elsewhere). In it, share how God is working in your marriage and watch as your story ministers to others. You never know who might read it and be encouraged.

GROUP STUDY LEADERS

If you would like to lead a small group based on this devotional, bulk discounts are available (8+ copies). Please e-mail details to care@fiercemarriage.com and someone will be in touch shortly.

SPEAKING REQUESTS

For speaking inquiries, please visit FierceMarriage.com/Speaking.

Notes

1. DAY 3: AN EXPERIMENT IN ANTIQUITY

The phrase, "buying up for yourselves the opportunity" comes from the *Expositors Greek Testament* translation of the Greek text behind "redeeming the time" (ἐξαγοραζόμενοι τὸν καιρόν). The complete *Expositors Greek Testament* commentary for Ephesians 5 can be found at: http://biblehub.com/commentaries/egt/ephesians/5.htm

2. DAY 9: HONESTY IS INTIMACY

Timothy Keller's words, "God invites us to come as we are, not to stay as we are," come from a post he made on Twitter, October 31, 2014, at 2:25 p.m., at @timkellernyc (https://twitter.com/timkellernyc/status/528296655859494912).

3. DAY 12: PARTNERING IN VISION AND FAITH

Matthew Henry's words, beginning, "When tossed and perplexed with doubts about the methods of Providence," come from his *Complete Commentary on the Whole Bible*, originally written in 1706 in six volumes.

4. DAY 18: AN OBVIOUS PURSUIT

Michael Hyatt's words, "I will speak often and lovingly of my wife. (This is the best adultery repellent known to man.)" come from his blog, MichaelHyatt.com, originally posted on Saturday, July 14, 2012, in a post titled "What are You Doing to Protect Your Marriage?" (https://michaelhyatt.com/what-are-you-doing-to-protect-your-marriage.html)

5. DAY 22: NO STRINGS ATTACHED

Gary Chapman's book, *The 5 Love Languages*, was first published in 1992, and is available from Chicago's Northfield Publishing in several editions.

6. DAY 25: PLAYFUL PURSUIT

Ralph Waldo Emerson's words, "It is a happy talent to know how to play," come from *Emerson in His Journals* (page 138) which was published by Harvard University Press on January 1, 1984.

7. DAY 31: CELEBRATING A LIFE OF PURSUIT

The quote from C. S. Lewis, beginning, "Duty is only a substitute for love (of God and of other people) like a crutch which is a substitute for a leg," is from *Letters of C. S. Lewis*, in a letter dated July 18, 1957, to Joan Lancaster. The collection is published by Harvest Books, copyrighted 1966.

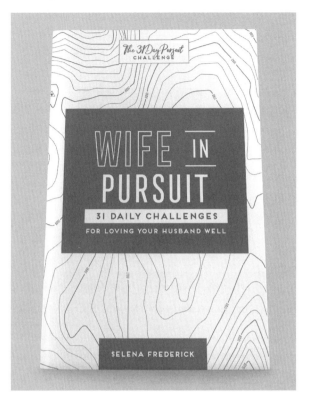

*Husbands, love your wives, as Christ loved
the church and gave himself up for her.*

EPHESIANS 5:25